ALWAYS NEVER
ALONE

A JOURNEY WITH THE HOLY SPIRIT

LEARNING TO KNOW HIS VOICE
EXPERIENCING GOD'S GLORY

CC HARVEY

ALWAYS NEVER ALONE
A Journey with the Holy Spirit

Copyright © 2022 CC Harvey

The scanning, uploading, and distribution of this book without permission is theft of the author's intellectual property. If you would like permission to use the material from this book, please contact ccharveyministries@gmail.com Thank you for your support of the author's rights.

www.ccharveyministries.com

ISBN: 978-1-7778-554-0-6
eBook ISBN: 978-1-7778-554-1-3

The stories in this book reflect the author's recollection of events. Some names, locations and identifying characteristics have been changed to protect the privacy of those depicted. Dialogue has been recreated from memory.

Book cover picture from [vivilweb]@123rf.com

Unless otherwise noted, all Scripture quotations are taken from the Holy Bible, New International Version, NIV. Copyright 1973, 1978, 1984 International Bible Society. Used by permission of Zondervan Publishers.

Scripture quotations are taken from the Holy Bible, New Living Translation (NLT). Copyright 1996, 2004, 2015. Used by permission of Tyndale House.

Publishers, Wheaton, Illinois 60189. All rights reserved. Scripture quotations marked KJV are taken from the Amplified Bible (AMP), copyright 2015 by the Lockman Foundation. Used by permission.

DOWNLOAD THE AUDIOBOOK FREE!

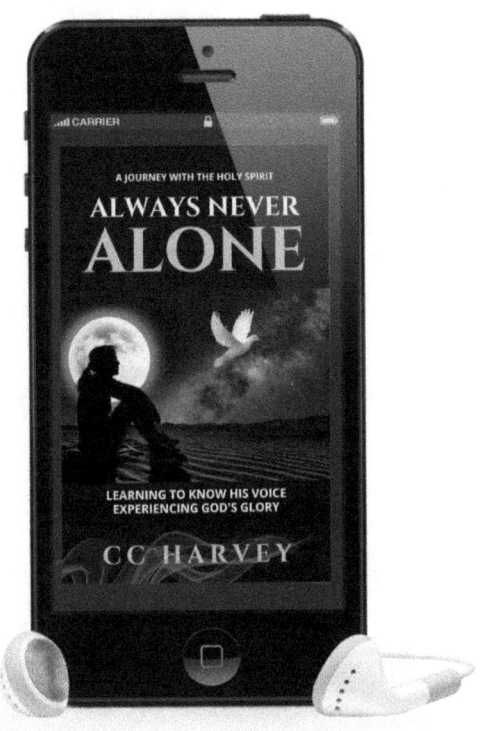

Thank you for purchasing my book. In appreciation, I would like to give you the audiobook version 100% Free!

https://www.ccharveyministries.com/freeaudio

(Password to enter is: neveralone)

DEDICATION

In memory of my brother Denis,
who left this world too early.

(June 19th, 1965 - May 20th, 1989)

TABLE OF CONTENTS

PREFACE ix
PART I – MY JOURNEY xi
Chapter 1:   My First Encounter with God 1
Chapter 2:   The Unseen World. 7
Chapter 3:   A Love for God. 11
Chapter 4:   God's Healing Power. 15
Chapter 5:   Domino Effect 17
Chapter 6:   High School 21
Chapter 7:   The Gift 25
Chapter 8:   Hard Work Pays Off. 29
Chapter 9:   Prophetic Word 31
Chapter 10: A Path Not Chosen. 33
Chapter 11: A Godly Intervention 39
Chapter 12: The Gift of Discernment 43
Chapter 13: Will I Breathe Again? 47
Chapter 14: A Light Amidst the Darkness 53
Chapter 15: Conquering the Fears 61
Chapter 16: Never Alone. 67
Chapter 17: A Message in Song. 75
Chapter 18: The Girl in the Picture Frame. 79
Chapter 19: The Lemon. 81
Chapter 20: End Time Dream 83
Chapter 21: Fibro Monster. 87
Chapter 22: "Airwaves" 91

Chapter 23:	Tuned in to God's Channel	95
Chapter 24:	My First Album Release	99
Chapter 25:	The Nail Clipper	103
Chapter 26:	Saying Goodbye	105
Chapter 27:	God Heard My Cry	109
Chapter 28:	Pursued by God	113
Chapter 29:	Infilling Power of the Holy Spirit	121
Chapter 30:	Closing the Boutique	133
Chapter 31:	Hungering for the Presence of God	137
Chapter 32:	Back to the Music	141
Chapter 33:	Wounded By Words	145
Chapter 34:	Angelic Intervention	153
Chapter 35:	Shook to the Core	157
Chapter 36:	End Time Song	161
Chapter 37:	End Time Music Video	165
Chapter 38:	When You Are Called	169
Chapter 39:	Finally Letting Go of the Pain	171

EPILOGUE **173**
ACKNOWLEDGEMENTS **177**
ABOUT THE AUTHOR **179**
CC HARVEY MINISTRIES **181**

PREFACE

My very first encounter with God was through a dream when I was ten years old. At the age of fifteen, I began to feel the call of God upon my life. I yearned for the gifts given by the Holy Spirit and had a deep desire to serve the Lord.

One day my father came home with a special gift for me, a guitar. The timing of that gift was no coincidence. It was perfectly orchestrated by God. Music would become an instrument to help me through the most challenging times of my life. Writing and composing music would help me pour my heart and draw closer to God.

In the 90s, I would begin to hear the soft whispers of the Holy Spirit in my mind, but would question myself time and time again. In times of great sorrow and imminent danger, the Holy Spirit would be there to comfort, guide, teach, and protect not only myself but those close to me. I would slowly learn to recognize His voice, become aware of His presence, and learn to obey as He guided me along the way. Through that wonderful friendship with the Holy Spirit, I would experience God's glory.

After a ten-year battle with fibromyalgia, I was miraculously healed in 2005 when God's tangible presence came upon me. Though I had received several healings in my life and felt God's presence, there was a time when selfish ambitions led me away from that closeness that I had with Him. I was the owner of a successful women's boutique, well known in the community, but something within me was missing. I had lost that inner peace and joy. I was a Believer, but at that time I consciously chose not to listen to the Holy Spirit. I knew He was there, but I lost myself in a world where self-validation through personal achievements and desire for money became more important. So, I submerged myself in retail fashion and enjoyed the financial successes that came along with it.

God would relentlessly pursue me, bring people, and circumstances my way to guide and gently lead me back into fellowship with Him.

In 2016, a three-hour encounter with God would forever change me, anchor me in a deeper relationship with Him through the Holy Spirit—I would never be the same! God would reveal Himself to me in such wondrous ways and lead me towards my calling.

Do you know God's voice? Are you tuned in to His channel? Are you missing that inner peace and joy in your life? Do you have difficulties overcoming the storms that come your way? Do you have a desire to get closer to God but find yourself distracted by the world around you? Do you feel God tugging at your heart? How do you know your calling?

As you read through the pages of this book, my hope is for you to find the answers to all these questions. My prayer is for you to have a better understanding of the Holy Spirit and how He communicates, and through that knowledge, have a closer, more intimate relationship with God. I pray that you experience the fullness of God's presence and all that He has for you as you walk moment by moment with the Holy Spirit.

This book is a personal recollection of the many encounters that I've had with the Holy Spirit. I will share with you the visions, the dreams, and the revelations given to me by the Holy Spirit in the hope that it broadens your understanding of what He does in a Believer's life, and how important He is to keep us anchored in Christ Jesus.

PART I

MY JOURNEY

CHAPTER 1

MY FIRST ENCOUNTER WITH GOD

"Carmen, are you ready? We are leaving for church in 5 minutes," yelled mother from the bottom of the stairs.

I grew up in Roman Catholicism. My family fervently went to church most Sundays, and on some occasions, my sister and I would go to Mass during the week. I loved the old smell of incense that permeated the air and the wooden pews with comfy kneelers. I always looked forward to kneeling on them during the sacraments. I never paid much attention to what the priest was saying since I was always looking around, fascinated by the splendor of it all; the stained-glass windows surrounding the sanctuary depicting the life of Jesus, the statues of the various saints and the stunning architectural design of the high ceilings.

A feeling of awe always swept over me whenever I entered the church. The presence of God would propel me to find the nearest pew and reverently get down on one knee and do the sign of the cross. I was very conscious of the existence of God. As a young child, Jesus was but a baby that I saw at Christmas time in a manger or as a statue in His mother's arms. I had no heart connection to the Jesus I saw on the cross. I didn't know anything about Salvation.

I was the second born in a family of four children. My sister Claire was two years older than me, followed by Denis and our younger brother Julian.

I always felt different as a child. So much so that one hot summer day, while sitting on the stairs of our backyard porch, I asked my mother if I was adopted. I had such a sad, worried look on my face. I was five years old at the time.

"Carmen, why would you think such a thing?" said mother with a puzzled look on her face. "Of course not! You're our little girl and we love you very much!"

Later in my teens, I would recall an instance where my mother said out of frustration: "Why can't you be like the others?" She meant, of course, my other siblings. She would later share with me, in her seventies, that I was indeed different because there was a feistiness about me that she did not see in her other children.

I had a wonderful childhood. I enjoyed playing knock the cans, hide and seek, and basketball with the other children in the neighborhood. As siblings, we always got along, apart from when I got into a fight with my brother Denis and accidentally gave him a bloody nose. My sister was quite moody in my early teens and liked to have her space. We shared a room, and I was the messy one, always scattering my clothes about. Father had to build a wall to separate our beds. Shortly after that, Claire decided to put tape across the floor to divide the rest of the room.

"Stay on your side of the room, and I'll stay on my side, and don't touch my clothes," she would say in her most authoritative voice. Even though I feared her, I didn't really stay on my side! I would get into trouble many times, especially when I wore her clothes. When she would find out about it, anxiety would well up within me. It was an awful feeling!

We had our differences, but we loved each other. At bedtime we had created our very own special knocking codes. Two knocks on the wall meant: "Goodnight." One knock meant: "Are you still awake?" It was our way of communicating with each other. It was endearing, and it made me feel in some strange way closer to her.

I loved doing things with my dad and enjoyed watching him renovate the house. Sometimes he would let me hammer a few nails or let me hold a two-by-four as he sawed.

My father had an excellent mind for business and was always busy doing something: buying and selling old cars, buildings, land, and more. He always had great ideas. He bought an old bus one year and converted it into a camper. We had some pretty amazing trips throughout Ontario in that camper bus.

As the owner and operator of a successful electrical contracting company, he worked long hours and often came home later in the evenings. Regardless, he would always take the time, even when tired, to play a game of catch with me. My parents loved each other very much, which was evident to us. Dad would always hold Mom's hand when they walked together, and we always saw that twinkle in their eyes when they looked at each other.

My mother didn't work outside of the house until we were teens. In those early years, it brought me much comfort to know that she was there when I arrived home from school. She had a lot of wisdom, and on several occasions gave me advice that would change the course of my life. I was eleven years old when Mother and I went for a short walk around the neighborhood. I still remember to this day, the name of the street where she gave me these words of advice:

"Carmen, you are getting quite mouthy. There are two roads in life that you can take: the right path or the wrong path. You are heading in the wrong direction." She was right; I was becoming quite sassy with people, especially with the neighbor that lived beside us. Those words spoken by my mother had a huge impact on me. From that day on, I became respectful of others and I learned to tame my tongue. God used my mother at specific times in my life to protect and guide me along the way.

Our home had a strong foundation of love and faith in God, and this was greatly reflected in the way that my parents lived. We learned to love, share, and care for one another. What was taught in our home poured out to others around us!

THE ASSAULT
-Summer 1970-

"Let the little children come to me, and do not hinder them, for the kingdom of heaven belongs to such as these." (Matthew 19:14, NIV)

It was a warm summer day in 1970. I was by myself, cheerfully playing outside, when someone I trusted—someone close to my family, sexually assaulted me. I was just seven years old.

The course of my life changed that day. A spirit of fear entered my very being. I began to have many suppressed fears and anxieties and often cried for no apparent reason. It was difficult for my parents to understand because they were completely unaware of what was happening emotionally inside of me.

I subconsciously buried the trauma of that day, but my wounded soul was crying out! I suffered from separation anxiety, especially when my parents left for several weeks on their yearly vacation. I would start to cry weeks before their departure. I also had an intense fear of change and growing up. I exhibited signs of post-traumatic stress, all of which were unknown to me or my parents. As a young child, I was too young to comprehend and explain what had happened—I never told anyone! It would take twenty-one years for me to speak to my mother about what happened and over fifty years to tell my father.

THE DREAM
-Summer 1973-

"The Lord is my rock, my fortress, and my Savior; my God is my rock, in whom I find protection. He is my shield, the power that saves me, and my place of safety."
(Psalm 18:2, NLT)

My first encounter with God happened when I was ten years old. I was nestled in bed when an intense fear of "being alone" swept over me. I eventually fell asleep, and during the night, God spoke to me for the first time through a dream. I was in outer space, surrounded by stars and planets. There was darkness, but I wasn't afraid. I knew that God was with me, and I felt at peace. God said to me: "If you had been the only one in the world, I still would have sent my Son to die for you. I love you and I will take care of you. You will never be alone—I will always be with you."

I did not comprehend the depth and significance of that dream until years later. I believe God spoke to me that night because of the deep, impenetrable hurt within my heart. In His loving kindness, God reached out and made me a promise that He would forever keep!

CHAPTER 2

THE UNSEEN WORLD

THE HAUNTED HOUSE

"For we are not fighting against flesh-and-blood enemies, but against evil rulers and authorities of the unseen world, against mighty powers in this dark world, and against evil spirits in the heavenly places." (Ephesians 6:12, NLT)

During my childhood and into my early teen years, my siblings and I encountered many supernatural occurrences in our home.

These experiences would further solidify within me the reality of the existence of a spiritual world.

One evening, while sitting at the kitchen table playing cards with my siblings, a potted plant on the counter began to move, then crashed onto the floor. We all looked at each other shocked, unable to speak or move for a few seconds—then frantically ran to the living room to hide behind the sofa.

"I'm not going out there," I whispered behind the sofa.

"I'm not either," said Denis with a frightened look on his face.

We stayed behind that sofa for quite some time.

"Well, I'm not going to stay here all night," said Claire as she courageously stood up and went to the kitchen to clean the mess. My sister was always the brave one.

At times, the utensils would rattle on their own in the drawers. It was terrifying for all of us. I don't know if my parents believed us because most of these unexplainable occurrences happened when they were sleeping or not at home.

At night, I always slept with my head under the covers. Sometimes, my brothers would see two ghostly figures during the night: one tall man wearing a top hat, and a shorter man with a melon hat. These ghostly manifestations greatly disturbed my brothers. One night, they decided to build a fortress of sheets around their bunkbed to stop seeing them. Unfortunately, this was a useless endeavor since the ghosts would poke their heads through the sheets to look at them.

My sister and I never saw those ghostly figures in our room; however, one night, a cold hand touched me as I slept with my right arm extended off the side of the bed.

Naturally, I started screaming! I was between sleep and wakefulness when my father came into the room and held me. I started flailing my arms and, in the process, accidentally punched him—I thought he was a ghost. My parents assumed that I was having a nightmare. I never did explain what happened.

When I was fifteen years old, my father built a new family home in the country, and I was pleased to leave those pesty ghosts behind.

What I experienced in that house, and many other occurrences while growing up, helped me to later understand as a Believer, that we battle in this physical world against unseen powers and principalities. This knowledge would make me aware of the presence of God to a greater extent.

CHAPTER 3

A LOVE FOR GOD

Sister Marguerite (right), and Cécile (middle), who would later become my grandmother, lived in the late 1930's in the Motherhouse of "Little Franciscans of Mary" in Baie-Saint-Paul, Québec. Sister Marguerite had been at the convent for many years. Her younger sister Cécile, in her early twenties, had been there for almost three years. She had completed the training, had progressed through the different vows to become a fully consecrated nun, but life was about to take her on a different journey. One day she received a call requesting that she return home to care for her ailing mother and look after the household. She would later meet a dashing older man named Délias. Before dying, her mother said, "Cécile, Délias is a good man. Promise me that you will marry him." Cécile fulfilled that promise and married my grandfather to be, even though she wasn't madly in love with him. Meanwhile her sister stayed at the convent to teach music.

    I have a few memories of Sister Marguerite visiting us when I was five or six. I was shy around her yet captivated by her clothing: the long black tunic with the white wimple and black veil on her head. The only skin that I could see was her face and hands. It was

quite strange to me. I didn't really understand why she wore all those clothes. She had a large silver cross around her neck that looked so heavy. She had a quiet disposition, and I remember feeling quite at peace with her. I don't remember conversing with her, but I can recall one time when she gave us a quarter to get candies at the corner store.

BELL BOTTOM JEANS
-Grade 6, 1976-

When I was eleven years old, I had a deep desire to devote my life to God and become a nun, just like Sister Marguerite. So, one day, I decided to meticulously embroider the word "God" at the bottom of my bell-bottom jeans with threads of different colors—it was my way of showing that I loved God.

I wore those jeans proudly to school one day, but sadly, two children from another class noticed the embroidery and started bullying me during recess. I was dumbfounded and felt lost for a moment until a few of my classmates came to my rescue. This incident disturbed me and made me realize that showing my outward love for God had consequences.

CHAPTER 4

GOD'S HEALING POWER

-Summer 1976-

I experienced for the very first time God's healing power when I was thirteen years old.

"Mom, I can't walk. My legs are hurting," I softly cried as I rubbed my knees.

I was having a lot of pain in my knees and lower legs that summer. The pain was so intense that I couldn't bear weight, I had to use crutches. My father had to carry me up the stairs to put me to bed. I couldn't even tolerate the weight of a blanket over my legs; I would start to cry.

My parents, who were becoming quite concerned, brought me to see our family physician. He immediately referred us to a specialist. Several months later, an arthroscopy was performed to determine if there was a problem with my knee joints, but no abnormalities were found.

One day, Aunt Yvonne came over to the house. She was a Believer in Jesus Christ and was part of the new Catholic charismatic renewal movement. The main concept of that movement was to experience the "baptism of the Holy Spirit" or "infilling power of the Holy Spirit," such as experienced by the one hundred and twenty people in the upper room at Pentecost. In the early Church, many were baptized and received healings with the laying on of hands.

I was standing in the kitchen, leaning forward on my crutches when Aunt Yvonne approached me with a warm smile.

"Carmen, can I pray for you?"

"Okay!" I replied with a half-grin.

As she gently lay her hands on me and prayed, I felt a slight tingling sensation, like electricity moving from the very top of my head down to my feet. I told my aunt what I had felt and then went outside to watch the other children play.

The following day, I sprang out of bed—the pain was gone! I was able to run and play basketball all day. I felt so happy to be free of the pain.

"Thank you, God," I softly whispered under my breath. "Thank you so much!"

Doctors were not able to find the root cause of the pain, but God, the Great Physician had healed me. He was looking out for me, just as He had said in that dream, but I was not yet conscious of that.

As my aunt lay her hands on me and prayed, the healing power of the Holy Spirit within her came unto me. She was sensitive to the leading of the Holy Spirit, and because of her obedience and faith, I was healed!

CHAPTER 5

DOMINO EFFECT

My Grandmother Cécile's oldest daughter, Aunt Yvonne, was a prayer warrior and was greatly used by God to bring many in our family to salvation. Grandma Cécile told me that she became a Believer in the mid-'70s while attending a church service with Yvonne. Shortly after my healing, my mother came to Christ, but my father had difficulty adjusting. "I was born Catholic, and I'm going to die a Catholic," he would continue to say with conviction.

Years later, my father attended a service at a Christian Pentecostal camp called "Silver Birches" in Chaput Hughes, Ontario. Uncle Mitch and Aunt Yvonne owned a cottage there, and my sister and I often went during the summer to help out at camp. That day, as I sat in the back of that little church, an alter call was made for those who wanted to accept Jesus in their hearts. To my surprise, I saw my father go up to the front with uncle Mitch. I was beyond excited! Regardless, my father would continue to profess that he was a Catholic, unbeknown to him that many Catholics were also Born-Again.

My sister Claire was invited to a service at the Salvation Army, which was a Church that Aunt Yvonne also attended.

During that service, my sister received the gift of salvation and became a Born-Again Believer in Christ. She was not the same person when she came home that day. I was angry at first because I didn't understand the sudden change. She was happy all the time. I was used to her moodiness, and she was nice to me for some unknown reason. I believed in God, but she had a joy that I didn't have, and I must admit, I was a little envious.

My two brothers also became Believers and came to Church with us every weekend. My father never came with us, but never complained about my mother attending.

Aunt Yvonne's faith in Jesus Christ created a domino effect that changed the lives of many in my family.

CAMP WASKESIU
-Summer 1977-

"Carmen, do you want to help us with the arts and crafts at camp for a week?" asked Anna over the phone. Anna was the coordinator for Camp Waskesiu, a children's camp run by the First United Church in Timmins, Ontario.

"Sure, it'll be fun!" I enthusiastically replied. I always enjoyed drawing, painting, and doing crafty projects. I enjoyed being around children and considered this to be an excellent opportunity. I was relieved when she told me that my cousin Dave would be there because, unknown to anyone, I suffered from anxiety. Dave would alleviate some of my worries since I did not know anyone there.

One sunny afternoon, as I stood under the shade of an old tamarack tree, a man read a Bible story to the children and shared about Jesus dying on the cross. I stood there attentively listening to everything said about Jesus and the gift of salvation. Something incredible happened! There was a stirring within me. I realized that I was a sinner, that there was nothing I could do on my own to stand righteously before God. Jesus, the man on the cross, seen as a child, became real to me. I knew that He was God, my Savior!

"Please Jesus, forgive me of my sins," I softly whispered. "I accept you as Lord and Savior. Come into my heart."

There was something different within me, an overflowing peace, and on that beautiful hot summer day, under the shade of an old tamarack tree, I accepted Jesus Christ as my Lord and Savior!

I now understood the joy seen in my sister Claire. I had that joy. I was "Born Again"—changed from within!

CHAPTER 6

HIGH SCHOOL

SET APART

"The world would love you as one of its own if you belonged to it, but you are no longer part of the world. I chose you to come out of the world, so it hates you." (John 15:19, NLT)

By the time I reached High school, many of my elementary school friendships had ended. Most of them enjoyed partying and I didn't feel comfortable in those settings. I always felt like God was watching over me. The few times that I did attend a school dance, I would say to myself: "If Jesus was to return right now, would this be where He would want me to be?"

I was shy and self-conscious, but it didn't stop me from participating in extracurricular activities such as public speaking, sports, and various school committees.

Studying became an escape from the world, a place to hide my fears. In the first two years of high school, I changed my handwriting almost every month and rewrote my notes all the time. It was something that I could control because I had a lot of anxieties. I lacked confidence in myself—I never thought I was good enough. So, this propelled me to excel academically. Many of my friends perceived me as a force to be reckoned with, but within me lay an emotional roller coaster.

In my last year of High School, I was Vice-President of Student Council, but I did not fit in with the most popular students. They respected me, but I felt apart from them. I knew from the Word of God that as a Believer, I was not of this world, that I had been set apart for His Kingdom. I felt that way—like an outsider looking in.

My cousin Dave, who was almost the same age, accompanied me to school every day. We had common interests; we loved God, ran together, and attended the same Youth Group. We were good friends! Everyone thought he was my boyfriend! That was a good thing; he was the perfect shield for me in those early years since I did not want to date at all. Dave was clueless about what had happened to me as a child, but God used Him to protect me.

YEARNING FOR THE GIFTS

"Follow the way of love and eagerly desire gifts of the Spirit, especially prophecy." (1 Corinthians 14:1, NIV)

Every Friday evening, cousin Dave, my sister Claire, and I would go to the Timmins Pentecostal Church to gather with other teenagers for Bible study and fellowship. While praising and worshiping God together, we would experience the joy, the peace of His presence.

Mark Wixson, our youth leader, preached the Word with great confidence. I could see God's anointing power upon Him as he prayed over people. There was a certain glow about him, and the workings of the Holy Spirit in and through him were evident. As I observed and listened, I began to have a yearning for more! I wanted what Mark had— the gifts of the Holy Spirit. I wanted to be used by God.

At the age of fifteen, the Holy Spirit blessed me with the gift of speaking in tongues. It was wonderful to pray and worship God in a heavenly language only known to Him. It strengthened and uplifted me spiritually and made me feel so special. Praying in tongues was "God and me" time!

God brought many wonderful Christian friends into my life at that time to guide, counsel, and protect me along the way, but I still had many hurts hidden deep within my heart.

God had a plan for my life and would be there in the storms that lay ahead.

MAY THE FORCE BE WITH YOU

I was fourteen years old in the summer of 1977 when I stood in line at the movie theater with my father to see the first episode of Star Wars.

Star Wars was not only about different characters living in a far-off Galaxy with droids and aliens, but it was also about light fighting darkness. What interested me about Star Wars was "the force" and how it manifested through Luke Skywalker and Jedi Yoda. I know this may sound strange, but it was through "Star Wars" that I started to understand the presence and power of God residing within me. I likened the Holy Spirit to "the force" in Star Wars.

I knew the transformative effect of God's presence in my life and what I had witnessed with my sister, but God wanted me to know much more about His Glory, which He would do later in my life. He would gradually prepare me for that.

CHAPTER 7

THE GIFT

-Winter 1979-

We moved into our new home on St. Patrick's Day, March 17th, 1979. It was such a blessing to live in the country. Each morning, we awoke to the sound of birds melodiously singing, and when I looked up from my bed, I would see trees often swaying in the wind through my window. I imagined them praising the Lord, and it made me feel happy inside.

Friends from our youth group would gather at the house almost every weekend to sing, play board games and take long walks in the country. There were great friendships, and we all had one thing in common, a love for Jesus.

There was always music in our home, especially when we traveled and camped in the summertime. We listened to many country and gospel artists, but I especially enjoyed listening to Elvis Presley, Jim Croce, and Keith Green.

One evening after work, my father came home with a musical instrument for each of my siblings. I received a guitar, and unbeknownst to me, this gift would be instrumental in helping me heal and overcome the many trials that lay ahead. That guitar was a seed planted by God, not only to pour out my pain but draw me closer to Him. I was sixteen years old when my father gave me that guitar, and from that day, I began writing and composing country and gospel music.

My brother Denis often sang and played the guitar with me, while my sister and I sang a cappella each evening as we washed and dried the dishes. It was a great time to practice our harmonies.

Grandma Cécile would come over every weekend and play classical music on our old piano downstairs. One key was always out of tune, but it never stopped Grandma from playing. She was amazing!

"Grandma, who taught you how to play?" I asked as I sat beside her on the piano bench.

"My sister taught me when I was at the convent. She was strict and would slap my hand every time I made a mistake," she casually replied as her fingers delicately danced over the keys. I was surprised by her response since she hardly spoke about those early years at the convent.

One day, I thought to myself, *I'll play just like her.* Grandma Cécile instilled in me a love for music that would stay with me forever.

FIRST PERFORMANCE
-Fall 1980-

I was seventeen years old when I performed my first original song at a local Pentecostal Church.

"I would like to invite Carmen to the pulpit to sing a song that she recently wrote called *Deep Down in the Valley*," said Pastor Deetz. I was nervous as I awkwardly picked up my guitar and headed towards the platform. I stood there in front of about one hundred people as my heart started pounding in my chest. I thought it would jump right out of me. Then, as I began to strum the guitar, I became more relaxed and got right into it. I pressed so hard on the fretboard while I played that I thought my fingers would bleed, but they were okay, just a bit red. Nonetheless, it was exciting and empowering for me to sing for the first time in Church. I proudly returned to my seat, beaming with joy as the congregation applauded.

"DEEP DOWN IN THE VALLEY"

Deep down in the valley lived an old man
This old man had a Bible
And he preached the Word of God
People from everywhere came to see this old man
But, then one day the old man died
And the people no longer came

Then one day a child went by
He saw the bible there
He opened it up and then he said:
"You people come to hear the Word
You're not coming for a man
You're coming for the Word
The Word is God and God is the Word
The Word is eternal life"

Deep down in the valley lived an old man
This old man had a Bible
That he found when he was a child
Through trembling hands, he passed the Bible
Throughout the generations
And eyes were opened, and souls were saved
And they all came to praise the Lord Amen… Amen…

Copyright 1980, CC Harvey music.

CHAPTER 8

HARD WORK PAYS OFF

I was in French public speaking competitions from grade six to grade twelve. Learning the skill of speaking was challenging and quite nerve-racking. Mr. Boisvert, my French teacher in High School, was an incredible coach but annoying at times.

He would always say to me: "You need to stop talking with your hands."

"Okay, I'll try my best," I would reluctantly reply. It was so frustrating because I always gestured with my hands when I spoke. I don't think it was because I was French, I was just a very expressive person, but Mr. Boisvert kept emphasizing that it was too distracting.

"Carmen, practice your speech with your hands in your pocket and concentrate on the tone and projection of your voice," Mr. Boisvert would say as he sat in the corner of the room with his arms crossed.

As we got closer to the date of the competition, Mr. Boisvert would bring out the VHS camcorder and video me as I practiced my speech. I hated seeing myself on screen, but I learned to stand straight and tall and control my hand movements and facial expressions.

A week before the competition, Mr. Boisvert would send me to various classes to say my speech. Anxiety would well up within me as I knocked on those classroom doors. There was a part of me that wanted to run away, play hooky, but I felt the fear, and did it anyway. It was not easy being in front of other students. Some laughed at my gestures, while others were captivated by what I had to say. I received a lot of feedback from students, which helped improve my skill.

I was always in second or third place in most of the competitions, but never first. By grade twelve, I started getting a little discouraged, but on February 18th, 1981, I was honored with first place in my division in the Royal Canadian Legion Branch 88 public speaking contest. Then, on March 19th, 1981, I became the zone winner. I was proud of myself that year because I worked so hard and was finally recognized. My parents were supportive and traveled with me all over Northern Ontario to compete. They were my greatest fans.

Public speaking gave me confidence in myself and helped me communicate better with people. I learned the art of being a good listener, addressing an audience, and capturing their attention.

All these years of practice and hard work had paid off. Unknown to me, public speaking would become an essential asset in my future.

CHAPTER 9

PROPHETIC WORD

-Winter 1981-

"What are we going to call ourselves?" said my sister Claire. After much deliberation, we all agreed on the name "Shine On." I was eighteen years old, the youngest member of a new four-girl band. I played the guitar and sang backup. Janice played the piano while Shelly and my sister Claire sang lead. We all got along quite well and diligently got together one day a week to pray and practice our songs. Our voices harmonized well with each other. Over time, we became known in our little community, and we started getting invitations to sing. God's anointing power was evident in our little group, and we took the responsibility of being God's stewards seriously.

One Saturday morning, we performed at a Full Gospel Businessmen's breakfast, and many were blessed as they felt God's presence while we sang. After the meeting, the girls began packing up the gear while I helped put the chairs away. I stood there in the middle of the room, surrounded by empty tables, when suddenly I felt disconnected from the world around me. It was as though I was inside of a picture frame looking out. I noticed an older man with short, thick white hair approaching me. I recognized Mr. Elmer Telford right away from his thick, black-rimmed glasses. Mr. Telford was a very well-known and respected man of God in our community. He gently took my hand and prophetically declared over me: "You will sing in front of thousands of people!"

I stood there speechless! *How did he know my heart's desire? How did he know that I wanted to be used by God?* I thought to myself. He then casually walked away, and that was that! The words spoken over me that day would profoundly impact my life. I would never reveal to anyone those prophetic words but would keep them safely tucked away in my heart. God had used Mr. Telford to reveal a part of my calling.

I left the band a year later because I no longer wanted to be a backup singer. Instead, I felt God's calling as a solo artist. I desired to write and compose music and sing the way I wanted to.

An end time song written in 1969 by Larry Norman kept drawing my attention during that time. The song was called: "I Wish We'd All Been Ready." When I heard this song for the first time, there was a stirring within me. I began to have a burden for people's souls. I knew that God was calling me to ministry; I sensed it every time I picked up the guitar and sang.

CHAPTER 10

A PATH NOT CHOSEN

I was about to graduate from high school, and the pressure was on to decide a career path.

"Carmen, you excel in sciences. I would strongly suggest that you choose a career that fits your strengths," said my guidance counselor. "A decision needs to be made soon if you want to start college or university in the fall."

I had spent many summers working for my father and decided that I wanted to follow in his footsteps and become an electrician.

"Dad, can I talk to you about something?" I said as I stepped into his office.

"What is it, Carmen?" he asked as he unrolled electrical plans on the table.

"I want to go to school to become an electrician."

Suddenly, my father stopped what he was doing, looked up, and with a serious frown said without hesitation, "No, Carmen, it's not a trade for a young lady."

"But Dad, I want to be an electrician!"

"No!" he quickly responded. "It's too physically demanding,

and the men in that trade are pretty rough."

I was shocked by his response, but knew that he was somewhat right. I had encountered some of those so called "rough characters" while working for my father, but many of them were very soft-hearted. In the early eighties there were not many women working as electricians, and those that were in the trade were not respected by many of the men.

"Okay, Dad. If I can't be an electrician, I'll go to university and become a doctor," I responded with a hint of frustration.

"Carmen, you're sick every year. You won't have the capacity, and it'll be a waste of money." I was so upset, but once again, he was right! I was always sick with the flu, sometimes a couple of times a year, or I'd get pneumonia. I wasn't born with a robust immune system.

"You'll find what is right for you," said my father reassuringly. A few months later, I was thrilled to receive a letter of acceptance to the three-year Nursing program at Northern College in South Porcupine, Ontario. It was not my initial chosen path, but since my sister was in Nursing, I decided to follow suit. My final clinical placement before graduation was on a surgical floor; therefore, when the hospital posted a full-time position for Surgical 3A, I was accepted right away because I had the experience. I graduated with a Diploma in Nursing and passed the exam in the summer of 1984.

I worked afternoon and night shifts most of the time. On one of those night shifts, while doing the rounds at two o'clock in the morning, I heard several horrible screams coming from one of the rooms on the adjacent men's surgical floor. Back then, we didn't have mixed wards.

"Who are you? What are you doing in my room? Don't come near me, get out, get out!" frantically screamed a man. *What on earth is going on*, I thought to myself. *It's two o'clock in the morning, and there are no visitors. He's in a single room.* Two nurses immediately ran into the room. I continued with my round, slightly shaken by what I had just heard.

The man who screamed passed away that night. *What happened in that room? What did he see? Was he saved?* I kept asking myself those questions. It bothered me—I was concerned about his soul.

After two years on the surgical floor, I transferred to First Medical. The pace was a lot slower than Surgical 3A but was more emotionally taxing since there was a lot of palliative care. My responsibility was to comfort, care and provide relief to those who suffered from pain and assist them with their daily activities. I often prayed silently for the clients when I worked, especially on the night shifts.

As a Nurse, I have witnessed the resiliency of the human spirit. I have learned compassion and love through the suffering of others. I have sat, listened, and cried, holding the hand of many in the silence of the night.

WALKING LIKE A PENGUIN

"On the count of three, Sharon, we're going to lift Mr. Johnson. Just hold the sheet under him," I worriedly said as he was slowly sliding down from his Geri chair.

"Sure, Carmen, I'm ready," replied Sharon.

Sharon was an older lady who had been away from nursing for several years and was a new hire on our floor.

Bending slightly forward, I widened my stance as I prepared to lift the client.

"One, two, three, lift," I said as I looked at my colleague, but she didn't lift. I immediately felt a burning sensation in my lower back. I returned to the nursing station, walking like a penguin.

"I just hurt my back," I told several of my co-workers as I bent forward to try to alleviate the pain. I was upset because this happened due to someone else's incompetency. The appropriate paperwork had to be filled out and reported. I was beside myself.

A few days later, I began having shooting pain down my right leg and throbbing pain in the lower sacral area of my back. My doctor advised me to be off work for two weeks and gave me a prescription for anti-inflammatory and pain medications. He also referred me to see Dr. Tortini, a local chiropractor.

"How long will it take for my back to heal?" I said to Dr. Tortini as I slowly and painfully got off the treatment table.

"The body responds differently to pain and you have sustained a lot of injury to the muscles and ligaments of your lower back. I will need to see you twice a week," replied Dr. Tortini.

It was a very difficult time for me. I had constant dull pain in my lower back, couldn't stand in one position for more than five minutes at a time, and couldn't pull, push, or lift anything over ten pounds.

It was hard for me to be still, and because of that, I returned to work a little bit earlier than I should have. I had been off for almost a month when I returned to the floor on light duty. That meant that I was to be careful and not lift anything heavy.

"Carmen, come and help us turn Mrs. Jones in room 320," said Judy, one of my co-workers. Mrs. Jones was over three hundred pounds.

"I can't lift," I replied. I felt useless, unable to help my colleagues, but I couldn't risk re-injuring myself.

"We need your help now," retorted my co-worker. I felt peer pressure. There were four other nurses in the room beside the client waiting for me to help, so I did. I felt a sudden burning, sharp pain in my lower back as I lifted. I returned once again to the nursing station, walking like a penguin. The injury was worse than before since I tore the muscles fibers that had previously healed. The hospital had no choice but to put me on a short leave of absence.

My recovery from the injury was extremely slow. Upon my return to First Medical, I applied for a transfer to the Intensive Care Unit and was accepted; however, my head nurse stopped the transfer, and I lost the position in ICU. As a senior nurse on the floor, I was needed to train all the new staff. I was very upset and so disappointed that I transferred to Porcupine General Hospital in South Porcupine, Ontario.

I continued to work at the PGH emergency department, but

my back continued to give me great difficulties. My injury was now considered "a chronic lower mechanical back injury." I knew that my career as a floor nurse was over; therefore, I applied to Laurentian University in Sudbury, Ontario, to pursue a degree in Liberal Sciences. My goal was to become a doctor.

I packed up my old silver Ford car and left for university in December of 1988.

CHAPTER 11

A GODLY INTERVENTION

OVERBOARD

In early May 1987, Peter (my future husband-to-be) was driving a 16ft aluminum boat with a 20hp outboard motor on Sturgeon Lake in Northwestern Ontario. It was a rather chilly day. Peter had his checkered wool coat on and heavy steel-toe work boots. His life jacket was tucked safely under the seat in front of him so that it would not blow away. It was a long two-hour journey to reach the drill crew on the lake. Peter started to get hungry along the way and decided to get his lunch from his backpack located on the seat in front of him. While leaning forward, his hand accidentally slipped off the tiller, causing the boat to turn sharply to the right, which propelled him over the left side of the boat into the icy cold lake. As Peter resurfaced, he was disoriented and started treading water. He slowly turned around and saw the boat driving away, travelling in in a circular path. "So this is how people drown!" mumbled Peter as he started feeling the coldness of the water on his body. He realized that one of two things would happen in the next few minutes: he could swim to intersect the boat as it made its way back to him and try to climb in, or the boat would pass out of his reach, and he would likely drown. There was no other option; drowning was a real possibility since he was a mile from shore. Swimming would be a challenge since the steel toe boots and the heavy clothes weighed him down. But he had no choice; he had to get on that boat! His body was already starting to get numb from the ice-cold water. It had been only a week since all the ice had melted off the lake. Time was running out! He began swimming to position himself to intersect the boat. He had but one chance, and he had to get it right the first time. As the boat approached, Peter aimed to grab it from the side.

"One, two, three," he muttered under his breath as he vigorously kicked his feet and latched himself to the side of the boat, trying hard not to capsize it. He managed to get his weighed-down body back into the boat and return to camp.

Peter later told me that he was not alone on that lake; he was given supernatural strength to get back into the boat. It was a miracle—it was a Godly intervention!

One year later, Peter was hired by a mining company in Timmins, Ontario. He moved not only because of the work, but deep within, he knew that he would find his soulmate—we met four months later.

THE HALO
-Summer 1988-

Dring! Dring! "Hello!"

"Hi Carmen, what are you doing tonight?" said my friend Sylvie. "I'm going to the Schumacher Day dance tonight. Do you want to come?" There was a long pause. "I'm busy tonight; I have to study for an exam that's coming up." It was an honest excuse since I was enrolled in a long-distance chemistry course for the summer.

"Come on, Carmen, you need a break from your studies," said Sylvie as she tried to make me change my mind.

After much persuasion, I finally gave in.

The "Schumacher Day" dance, an annual event held at the McIntyre Arena in Schumacher, Ontario, was usually well attended. The doors opened at eight o'clock that night, and we arrived shortly after that. There was loud music mixed with the cacophony of hundreds of voices. I awkwardly stood there in the middle of the arena with Sylvie. People were dancing all around us. I felt out of place as I held on to my drink. I don't know why I ordered an alcoholic beverage; I guess I was trying to fit in or thought it would help me relax a little. Nonetheless, I had a strong dislike for it.

Two young men engaged in conversation stood several feet in front of us. The tallest of the two was casually standing there with a beer in one hand. I was drawn to him as I noticed a bright, opal-colored halo around his entire body. I pointed my finger in his direction and confidently said:

"Sylvie, I'm going to ask that guy to dance."

As I started walking in his direction I stopped mid-way. I hesitated because, deep down I was afraid of being rejected. I was about to turn around when Sylvie annoyingly said: "I knew you wouldn't do it. Why don't you come out from under your shell?"

Did she just say that to me? I thought to myself. I was now determined more than ever to prove her wrong and show her that I had some spunk, so I walked right up to that young man and, without hesitation, said, "Would you do me the honor of this dance." *Who speaks like that?* I thought to myself, I did, and he said yes! God used Sylvie that night to fire me up!

Peter was a real gentleman. He never left my side that evening. He would later confide that he didn't want to lose me. As he walked me to my car, I told him that I was a Believer. He was very receptive, and I could see much kindness in his eyes.

"Robin, you won't believe this, I found her!" said Peter as he called his best friend the following day.

A NEW DOOR OPENS

Summer was coming to an end, and I was leaving soon for Laurentian University, three and a half hours away from my hometown.

In late August, Peter mentioned that Northern College in South Porcupine had posted a position for a bilingual nursing instructor. South Porcupine was ten minutes away from Timmins. We both knew that a long-distance relationship would be difficult. The timing could not have been better. So, by the grace of God, I applied and was hired as a full-time instructor in the Bilingual First Year Nursing Program. It was a miracle that I got the job since I only had half my degree in Liberal Sciences completed and had no prior teaching experience. Public speaking and my years in Medical/Surgical nursing had prepared me for this position.

My father was in the driveway, taking his heavy tool pouch out of his truck as I approached him.

"Dad, I have something to tell you. I'm not going back to university," I anxiously said. "I was hired by Northern College to teach in the nursing program. Are you disappointed?" I was old enough to make my own decisions, but I always respected my father's advice and I wanted him to be proud of me.

"Carmen, it doesn't matter what you do in life, as long as you're happy. I have always been proud of you."

A weight lifted from my shoulders. Becoming a doctor was not meant to be, and meeting Peter was no coincidence; it was a Godly intervention. God knew what lay ahead and knew we would be there for each other.

CHAPTER 12

THE GIFT OF DISCERNMENT

"There are different kinds of spiritual gifts, but the same Spirit is the source of them all. There are different kinds of service, but we serve the same Lord. God works in different ways, but it is the same God who does the work in all of us. A spiritual gift is given to each of us so we can help each other. To one person, the Spirit gives the ability to give wise advice; to another, the same Spirit gives a message of special knowledge. The same Spirit gives great faith to another, and to someone else the one Spirit gives the gift of healing. He gives one person the power to perform miracles, and another the ability to prophesy. He gives someone else the ability to discern whether a message is from the Spirit of God or from another spirit. Still another person is given the ability to speak in unknown languages, while another is given the ability to interpret what is being said." (1 Corinthians 12:4-10, NLT)

I had the gift of discernment early in my life, but I didn't know what it was. I believe that God prepared me for this gift and calling even before I was born. I was very sensitive to the spiritual world and experienced many unusual manifestations as a child. In my late twenties, this gift by the Holy Spirit would make me see and sense things that others could not. As a teenager, I began to have a heightened awareness of God's presence. The gift of discernment enabled me to see people's hearts and know if what they were saying was true or not. I would know if a Believer was saying something that came from God, Satan, or from their own minds. I was very sensitive to the presence of evil spirits.

In March of 1989, I went on a business trip to Montreal with a co-worker. We were walking through a convention center when a well-groomed youthful middle-aged man beckoned my friend to his booth. I instinctively decided to follow her. As we approached his booth, my spidey senses began to tingle. I noticed his lifeless, cold black eyes and the occultic merchandise displayed on the table. I knew that I needed to get Louise away from him. I felt a heaviness like a thick blanket wrapping itself around me, closing in on me. I knew within my spirit that there was darkness, an evil presence.

"We're not interested! Let's get out of here!" I blurted out as I grabbed my colleague's hand and abruptly walked away. It felt a bit awkward as I explained to Louise why I hastily pulled her away, but to my surprise, she understood and was quite thankful. She later confided in me that she was Catholic and believed in God.

The gift of discernment is essential to warn us when there is danger or something not quite right in our surroundings. It protects us from being led astray by false teachings. This gift protects the Believer by helping them see with spiritual eyes to know when an evil presence is around.

I often felt different, set apart from others, but this gift protected and helped me to know what was going on in different situations. Later in life, I would be cursed and offended by leaders in the church and be shunned by many Believers because they struggled to understand or receive what I discerned; they misunderstood me.

    I have learned from the Holy Spirit when to speak and when not to. There are times when the Holy Spirit will reveal something to me about someone, but it is for me to pray for them. Not everything has to be said to people. The gift of discernment is very important, but I believe that every Believer who has grown in their faith know, even without this gift, what is from God, and what isn't.

CHAPTER 13

WILL I BREATHE AGAIN?

LOSS OF A BROTHER
-Friday before May long weekend of 1989-

My parents owned a lovely cottage on Kenogamissi Lake, west of Timmins, Ontario. Peter and I decided to spend the weekend there. It was a cool, crisp summer day with a few dark clouds dispersed on the horizon.

My brother Denis had come for a short visit with his dog. He was very quiet, not his usual self that day. I felt an uneasiness from within as I watched him paddle away from shore with his dog in the canoe, but I just dismissed the feeling.

The whole family was at the cottage that day with all the grandchildren. Most of us were in the cottage playing games, enjoying each other's company. We were not expecting that many people for dinner, and I recall reluctantly sharing half of my hamburger with my brother Denis. Regardless, it was nice that we were all together! Denis went home later that night since he planned to go fishing with Julian the next day.

I woke up Saturday morning with a strong desire to go back home. I felt a restlessness within, like something was not right. I ignored the feeling. I should have prayed, but it never crossed my mind because I had never experienced a feeling like that before. That day, I stayed at the cottage but decided to leave shortly after dinner.

Around 7:00 p.m., I returned to my apartment and received a call from my brother's fiancée.

"Carmen, it's Melinda. I am here with Julian at your parent's house. Something happened to Denis. Is Peter with you right now?"

"No, Peter is gone home. What happened to Denis?" I said as I anxiously held on to the telephone.

"Denis is dead; Julian and I found him in the garage. Carmen, Denis is dead!" said Melinda, choking back tears. "Carmen are you there? Carmen!"

"What do you mean he's dead? I saw him yesterday. What do you mean? What happened?" I frantically yelled back. "No!" I screamed out loud as I collapsed onto the floor in a sitting position. Sobbing uncontrollably, I stared blindly at the ceiling in the living room. I could hear the traffic outside and the noise coming from the apartment next door, but nothing felt real.

Peter arrived at my apartment within minutes and held me tightly in his arms. His presence gave me strength as we drove to my parent's house. My brother Julian was sitting on a chair in front of the house, staring blankly ahead. He didn't speak to us at all. It was apparent that he was in shock. The police were there, along with the paramedics. A lot of the memory of that night escaped me, but I do remember that Peter did not want me to see my brother's body. A part of me desperately wanted to see him, but I realized later that it would have traumatized me. Peter was protecting me.

We were all in shock and disbelief as Peter, Melinda, and I drove silently into the night to see my parents at their cottage. The drive there felt like an eternity. I silently sat in the back of the car, pleading for God to bring my brother back; then I heard a voice from within say: "No, do not pray, he is with Me." As I listened to this voice, I had a vision in which I saw two gates of heaven close.

I would later share with my parents the words that I heard that night and the vision given to me. In their grief, it would bring them much comfort.

It was pitch black when we arrived at the cottage. All I could see was the silhouette of my mom silently crying outside on the deck. My parents had received the news from Uncle Mitch earlier in the evening. My sister Claire was at the cottage with her two young children. We prayed and comforted each other. We knew that the days ahead would be difficult ones. My parents were so strong—you could see God's peace in them. I couldn't feel anything; it was hard for me to fully grasp what had happened.

We left the cottage around two in the morning. Peter stayed with me that night and held me as we lay in bed, but I couldn't sleep; I couldn't stop the tears. I felt empty inside, as though someone had ripped out my heart—a pain so deep within my soul that I thought I would never be able to breathe again!

I was never angry with God when my brother passed; instead, I blamed myself for not doing enough, not seeing the signs, and they were all there, right in front of me!

Several months earlier, my brother had invited me for breakfast at a local restaurant. While there, he confided in me that he would take his own life.

"Denis, you can't do that," I blurted out, as I sat there in silence, stunned by his words. "You know that it will devastate

Mom and Dad, the family, your children," I softly said as I gazed at the cup of tea in front of me. Words escaped me.

"Yes, Carmen, I know, I'm not going to do that," Denis said reassuringly. "I'm okay; it was just a fleeting thought."

I knew that he was under the care of a psychiatrist, yet something was bothering me. I confided in a colleague at work but didn't think much about it as the weeks went by. Denis and I spoke on the phone almost every night, and he was so in love with Melinda. He was so happy! Why would he even think about taking his own life?

The month before his passing, Denis had given me his favorite fringed leather jacket and a beautiful Easter card. He had written one line in the card:

Thank you for all the wonderful times we've had. Much later, I realized that it had been written in the past tense.

A few weeks before his passing, the family had gathered at my parent's house in the country. Denis and I went for a bit of a walk around the property. I was troubled that day because my brother had almost lost his life the month before.

Denis worked for my father and was an accomplished electrician. One day while at work he accidentally electrocuted himself while working on a panel. The jolt was so intense that it threw him off the ladder. He was taken to the hospital and admitted to the intensive care unit for several days. I was so concerned about my brother, especially for his soul.

"Denis, do you love Jesus?" I said, trying to hold back tears. I was very troubled. "You almost died! Are you okay?"

"Yeah, I'm okay! You know I love Jesus," said Denis without any hesitation.

Nothing more had to be said. I knew within my heart that he was saved, and for some unknown reason, it was the reassurance that I needed.

Unbeknownst to me, my brother had tried to take his life when he electrocuted himself. The guilt of my brother's death would haunt me for years.

SAYING GOODBYE

I begged my dad not to have an open casket. "Please, Dad, I don't want to see Denis like that. I want my last memory of him to be one of him alive."

"Carmen, it's important for all of us to see him one last time and say our goodbyes," said my father in a gentle tone. "We need to have closure."

I tried to be strong as I approached the casket, but my heart was silently breaking into a thousand pieces. Denis looked so angelically peaceful, as though in a deep sleep. I wished that I could shake his shoulders and wake him up. *Wake up Denis, please wake up!* I gently kissed his cold forehead and slipped my favorite birthstone ring into his lifeless hands. I wanted to leave a part of me with him.

"This is not goodbye. I'll be seeing you again, bro!" I softly said under my breath. Then, I turned and walked away as tears rolled down my cheeks.

Over one hundred people came to my brother's funeral to say their goodbyes and offer their love and support. My family went through much pain and sorrow during that time, but we found strength in God and each other.

Denis would have turned 24 in June of that year. We usually celebrated our birthdays together since we were born the same month but four days apart. I was very close to Denis; his passing would leave a big emptiness in my heart.

CHAPTER 14

A LIGHT AMIDST THE DARKNESS

PROPOSAL
-July 9th, 1989-

Peter held my hand as he walked me home later in the evening. I noticed that his hand was clammy, and I could feel that he was nervous about something. I opened the door to my apartment and walked in, while he just stood there in the doorway.

"Carmen, can I come in for a glass of juice," said Peter in a rather serious tone, which was unlike him.

"Sure! Come on in," I answered as I looked inquisitively at him. He was behaving strangely. I knew he had something on his mind that he needed to share. As we both sat on the couch, he reached into the left side pocket of his pants and took out a small black velvet box.

"Carmen, I love you! Would you do me the honor of becoming my wife," he nervously said as he opened the box, revealing a stunning three-stone diamond ring.

"Yes, yes, I will!" I joyously cried out as I wrapped my arms around him. I immediately called my parents to share the good news. They were so excited!

We had the pain of my brother's death, but now the celebration of an upcoming wedding in October of that same year. The timing could not have been better! Despite my joy, I had moments of extreme sorrow.

It was late August, three months following my brother's death, when I returned to the College. I had a new curriculum for the Fall, which included teaching biology. I was surprised since I never thought that this opportunity would be given to me. It was a subject that really interested me. This was such a blessing, but instead of rejoicing, I sat at my desk and silently cried, unaware that one of my colleagues was in the room.

"Carmen, you shouldn't be here," said Marilyn as she gently put her hand on my shoulder.

"I know; I miss my brother so much. It's too soon! I am so overwhelmed right now!"

"You need to speak to the Director; she will understand. You need time to heal."

Yes, I needed more time. My brother's passing, the wedding, and the new curriculum were too much for me to handle. I had no choice but to take a short leave of absence because I was falling into a depression.

GOD HAS EVERYTHING IN CONTROL

Peter was not a Believer; however, he had heard the message of salvation at some point in his life.

I approached the new pastor of our church regarding our desire to be married in October, but to my surprise, he said: "Carmen, I will not perform the wedding ceremony because Peter is not a Believer."

I couldn't believe that he was refusing to marry us. I knew what Scripture said about "not being unequally yoked," yet I knew that God had brought us together. I was troubled. *What am I going to do? I love him!* I thought to myself. I had seen the halo, a sign given to me by God when I met Peter. I knew that we belonged together. I was beside myself, not knowing what to do. Meanwhile, Peter and I scheduled a meeting with a pastor from another church.

Pastor Cuzar was sitting behind his desk as we stepped into his office.

"Welcome, please take a seat," he said, gesturing with his hand. He was a charming man with a certain gentleness about him.

"I understand that you both want to marry," said Pastor Cuzar with a warm smile, which I believe was a trademark of his personality. We sat across from him and explained our situation. He was so patient and kind as he spoke to Peter about Jesus. He took a paper and drew a bridge between Jesus and God.

"Peter this is Jesus; He is the key for you to cross that bridge to God. When Jesus died on the cross, He took upon Himself the sins of mankind. He paid the price for your sins and became the ultimate sacrifice for you to be able to have eternal life with God. You see, God has nothing to do with darkness; sin. We have all fallen short in our lives because we have all sinned. When you believe that Jesus is God's Son, that He died for you on that cross, and you ask Him to forgive you of your sins and make Him Lord of your life, you become a child of God. Only through the shed blood of His risen Son can you cross that bridge and stand righteously before God. Jesus is the key!"

Peter sat there and listened attentively to every word he spoke. The pastor of my church had refused to marry us but agreed to let Pastor Cuzar officiate our wedding in the church.

-August 1989-

"Carmen, I have something to tell you," Peter said as he was driving. "I accepted Jesus in my heart."

"What?" I was dumbfounded.

"Yes, I understood what the pastor was saying. I accepted Jesus last night," said Peter looking straight ahead.

"Praise the Lord! Peter, I am so happy! Are you sure? You know how much this was troubling me."

Peter grinned, "Yes, I know, Carmen. I love you very much, but I did this for myself. It was something that I needed to do."

Beaming with joy, I felt the peace of God's presence as I sat beside Peter. God was indeed in total control of everything.

WEDDING
-October 6th, 1989-

It was during my depression that Peter and I married. We had a beautiful wedding with over two hundred people in attendance. I had invited many of my nursing students to the dance, and to my my surprise, they all showed up! It was heartwarming and enchanting all at the same time! There was great joy, but within me lay a shadow of grief, unbeknown to anyone. I desperately wanted my brother Denis to be there celebrating with us. I therefore imagined him at times in the room with us. Those fleeting thoughts of him brought me much comfort on our special day!

The following day we departed for Jamaica. It was a wonderful week of glorious sunrises over the crystal-clear water of that beautiful island paradise. We visited sugarcane plantations and participated in many activities while learning about Jamaican culture. One evening, as I was standing on the beach watching the sunset over the horizon, a feeling of loneliness and anxiety came over me. I knew that I loved Peter, but I questioned whether I had made the right decision in marrying so soon after my brother's death. As soon as that thought entered my mind, Peter came from behind and wrapped his arms around me.

"I love you!" he whispered in my ear.

At that moment, I knew that everything would be alright. I had peace within me and knew that we were not alone—God was guiding and protecting us.

GOD SPOKE THROUGH MY DAD

I returned to work in December of 1989 but still struggled with depression. My grief was so profound that it took its toll on me—I was emotionally and physically tired.

There was so much going on in my life after my brother's death that I never had the time to be still enough to go through all the stages of grief: denial, anger, bargaining, depression and acceptance. I was still in the depression stage.

At that time, music became my refuge, a way for me to pour my heart out to God. It pulled me away from the darkness of my grief and drew me closer to Him. God was my beacon of hope through the storm.

During the first few months of our newly married life, I frequently visited Grandma Cécile. She enjoyed reading the Bible and often wrote scripture verses and prayers to encourage me. One day she wrote me a verse from **Isaiah 40:31, NIV: "But those who hope in the Lord will renew their strength. They will soar on wings like eagles; they will run and not grow weary. They will walk and not be faint."**

Grandma wanted me to know that God would always be there to give me the strength that I needed. He would make me rise above the many storms. During that difficult time of my life, she wrote this prayer, which I translated from French.

"Lord God, my Father whom I love. You who see everything. Despite the pain in my heart and body, you know what I am going through. I love the designs of your Divine Providence on me and those who are dear to me. Lord be my strength, my light and help me find a solution to the problems that cause my distress. I thank you, my God!"

Grandma understood my pain since she suffered at times from depression. She had married a man she hardly loved who was an alcoholic. There were many challenging times, especially taking care of a home and raising five children on her own. Grandma's strength came from God and reading the Word. Through her children, grandchildren, and great-grandchildren, love found its way!

In April of 1990, I surprised my father at work.

"Hi Dad!" I said peeking through the half-closed door of his office.

"Hey, Carmen, come on in! How's my girl today?"

When I heard those sweet words, I sat down and started to cry. My father had a way of tugging at my heartstrings.

"Carmen, I don't like seeing you like this. You must go on with your life! Denis would not want you to be like this," sternly yet lovingly said my father.

His words echoed in my mind. It was as though God was speaking directly to me through him. The grief within me suddenly lifted, and by the grace of God, I was set free from the depression.

A BLESSING FROM GOD

On August 14th, 1990, our beautiful son was born at 5:05 p.m., weighing eight pounds, twelve ounces. He was twenty-one inches long and was born with a full head of black hair. Three months into my pregnancy, the Holy Spirit had told me to call him John, and so we did! We named him John Denis Harvey. The Hebrew name for John is **Yochanan**, meaning YAHWEH (God) is gracious.

A few days after his birth, my parents came to visit us. As my Mother held John in her arms, Dad softly said, with tears in his eyes: "He looks just like Denis!"

When I look back, I am so grateful to God! He had not only brought Peter into my life but blessed us with a son who looked a lot like my brother Denis.

Through my grief, God had continued to make His presence known to me. He had been a light amidst the darkness. The birth of our newborn son was a blessing and a sign that God was looking after us.

CHAPTER 15

CONQUERING THE FEARS

"The thief (the enemy) comes only to steal and kill and destroy; I have come (Jesus) that they may have life and have it to the full." (John 10:10, NIV)

A week after our son was born, I had postpartum depression (PPD). I didn't tell anyone what I was going through because they would have admitted me to a psychiatric unit. I knew that giving birth caused hormones to be off-balance, so I attributed many of my anxieties and suicidal thoughts to that. The postpartum depression was "the straw that broke the camel's back." Because of one trauma after the other, the invisible wall of defense within me began to crack and crumble. I started having an intense fear of dying, of going to hell, and a fear of losing someone. I didn't want to lose anyone close to me because I had lost a brother. I knew how devastating it was, and I don't think I would have coped with losing another person in my life. The fear of death and going to hell were constantly on my mind. It was unbearable!

The emotional pain repressed from the assault experienced as a child began to surface. I was angry and grieved the loss of my innocence, the loss of who I could have been. Though God had been there for me and had blessed me greatly, I resented that it had changed the essence of who I was supposed to be. It had filled me with anxieties and had robbed me of so much because I was afraid of life. I became very protective of our son, so I did not trust anyone with him, apart from my family.

Through those times of great difficulties, I wrote "Emotions." This song would help me pour out as I cried out to God for help—for healing.

"EMOTIONS"

Emotions wrapped up deep inside
Protecting myself from the pain
Pieces and puzzles remain
In a world of silence to be
Walls come tumbling down
Will I survive this time 'round?
People see what they want
And turn their eyes from the truth

Who will take away the pain?
Who will take away the shame?
Melt away these ashes from my heart
And let me love again
Let me love again

Light of God, shine through
Holy River, cleanse my soul
Set me free…. Set me free
You took away the pain
You took away the shame
You melted these ashes from my heart
And filled me with your love
You filled me with your love

I'll never be the same
You filled me with your love You
filled me with your love

Light of God, shine through Holy
River, cleanse my soul
Set me free…. You set me free
I'll never be the same
Your love…. Your love set me free

Copyright 1989, CC Harvey Music.

Aunt Yvonne was always there to counsel and pray for me. She had a lot of wisdom in spiritual warfare and would give me scriptures to read.

One day, as I was cleaning the house, the Holy Spirit said to me: "Carmen, when you gave birth to John, you didn't know what to expect, but you went through it. So, when it's time for you to die, you will go through it, and it's going to be okay because I'll be with you." The Holy Spirit reassured me that all would be well, and, in so doing, the fear of death gradually left me.

The scripture that comforted me the most during that season of my life was **Psalm 23, NIV:**

"The Lord is my shepherd, I lack nothing. He makes me lie down in green pastures, he leads me beside quiet waters, he refreshes my soul. He guides me along the right paths for his name's sake. Even though I walk through the darkest valley, I will fear no evil, for you are with me; your rod and your staff, they comfort me. You prepare a table before me in the presence of my enemies. You anoint my head with oil, my cup overflows. Surely your goodness and love will follow me all the days of my life, and I will dwell in the house of the Lord forever." (NIV, a psalm of David)

Through this passage of scripture, I understood that God would always protect and be with me through the trials. He would have His hand upon my life and would be there to guide and comfort me. I would always feel His presence and anointing upon my life. He would protect, rescue me from the enemy of my soul, and one day bring me home to live with Him forever.

My greatest battle during that time of my life was the one taking place within my mind. The emotional wounds within me gave access to the enemy. So much so that I was tormented daily by intrusive thoughts. I believed the lies that I was going to hell and that I wasn't saved. I felt that I was not good enough. My battles were not only emotional, but they were also spiritual.

My deliverance of those fears came about through prayers, through the Word of God—they were my spiritual weapons.

When I began to read more of God's Word, I gained wisdom from the Holy Spirit. I understood that His presence within me was my Guarantor of eternal life with Christ. **(Ephesians 1:14)** The same power that raised Jesus from the dead was living in me. That knowledge to me was incredible! I could have peace; I could walk victoriously as a child of God with the help of the Holy Spirit. The Word clearly states that **"God has not given us the spirit of fear; but of power, and of love, and of a sound mind." (2 Timothy 1:7, KJV).** When I realized all of that, the fears of dying and going to hell were gone forever. I experienced a release, a freedom from within.

There is so much power in the Word of God. Jesus says in **John 8:32, KJV: "Ye shall know the truth and the truth shall make you free."** With knowledge of the Word, came the release of my fears. My thoughts were no longer the same; my mind started to be renewed by the Word through the Spirit of God dwelling within me.

When I forgave my brother for taking his life by suicide, when I forgave myself, I was able to let go of the guilt, of the pain. I knew that I was loved by God even more because it says in His Word in **Psalm 147:3, NIV: "He heals the broken-hearted and binds up their wounds."**

I understood who I was in Christ—a daughter of a King who loved me, who had given His life to set me free. I knew that

He was there for me and that He would always have my back! The Holy Spirit became my best friend. I could trust him and bare my soul. He knew my deepest sorrows.

Letting go of the emotional pain from my childhood was not easy— it would take years. God took away my fears of death and hell, the pain of the loss of my brother, but I was not ready to surrender all to Him. I was able to forgive the one who assaulted me as a child, but I still held on to the pain, the memory of what happened.

God gives us the grace through the transformative power of the Holy Spirit to forgive those who have hurt us. There are times when the wounds within our hearts are so deep that they can take longer to heal, often due to our own unwillingness to surrender them all to God. I kept those wounds hidden in the deepest corners of my heart. Unfortunately, those wounds would eventually re-surface and affect me on a physical and emotional level.

I returned to teach at Northern College in January of 1990. John was now five months old. Women back then didn't have long maternity leaves like we have today. I had a hard time being away from my son. When I was at work, I wanted to be home; I didn't want to miss any of the developmental changes in him. After the semester, I resigned from my position and became a stay-at-home mom. I never regretted that decision.

To bring in extra income, I started selling a clothing line through home parties during the evenings. I really enjoyed helping women to feel good about themselves, and I did that through clothing and jewelry. I eventually started recruiting women to become independent sales consultants, and eventually had a team of ten ladies. I would do about two to three shows a week, and it was great because I was able to be home full-time during the day and have a social life—connect with other adults, which was very important to me. I now had that balance.

CHAPTER 16

NEVER ALONE

"Do not be afraid or discouraged, for the LORD will personally go ahead of you. He will be with you; he will neither fail you nor abandon you."
(Deuteronomy 31:8 NLT)

In the nineties, I started to hear the Holy Spirit speak to me as a soft whisper in my mind. I would question myself time and time again, but through different encounters, I would slowly learn to recognize His voice. The following events are a recollection of these wonderful encounters.

THERE IS ANOTHER
-Friday, November 8, 1991-

The snow was gently falling as my husband and I arrived at our favorite Chinese restaurant on the other side of town. It was our date night, and we were looking forward to some alone time together.

I was three months pregnant at the time, and during dinner, I started bleeding a little. Alarmed, we hastily left the restaurant and went immediately to the hospital. I was escorted to a private room and examined by the attending doctor on call.

It was a beehive of activity in the emergency department. All the nurses were scurrying about, taking care of many sick people.

"There's nothing we can do for you, Mrs. Harvey," said the doctor as he finished his examination. "The bleeding has stopped. I would strongly suggest that you go home and rest for the next couple of days."

I just lay there in bed with a perplexed look on my face. I was really concerned. I never bled with my first pregnancy. *Why didn't the doctor do more?* I thought to myself. I understood that they were busy, I was a nurse once, yet I felt like they could have done more. I felt helpless.

"Carm, everything is going to be okay. Let's go home," said Peter as he gently took my hand and helped me off the stretcher.

That night, I dreamed of a little girl about four or five years old with blonde, shoulder-length ringlets. She looked like Shirley Temple, a child actress from the thirties that I watched on television when I was younger. She was wearing a short, light blue, puffy-sleeved dress with patent black leather shoes with dainty white socks. She was holding my brother's hand. I knew that it was Denis because I recognized the tan jacket he often wore. They both had their backs to me, but she turned slightly around and waved goodbye with a big, bright smile on her face. She looked so happy!

During the weekend, I rested as best I could. I was a little concerned about what had happened Friday evening but did not let it consume my thoughts.

I awoke early Monday morning. It was November 11, 1991, Remembrance Day. Our son John, who was now fifteen months old, was busy playing with his toys as I vacuumed the kitchen floor. I suddenly felt a gush between my legs. I held my belly and dropped to my knees. Bright red blood was all over the front of my gown. I was in shock, unable to move as I stared blankly ahead. John ran and jumped on my belly as he wrapped his little arms around my neck, awakening me from my stupor. It was comforting to have him by my side. With trembling legs, I stood and walked towards the telephone. My hands were shaking so much that it was difficult to punch in the numbers. We had touch-tone phones back then. I couldn't reach my husband at work, but I was thankful that my dad was home. He called 911 right away.

The paramedics arrived and put me on a stretcher. My Dad held little John in his arms as they lifted me into the ambulance. I could see tears welling up in his eyes. I wanted to cry, but I had to be strong. I didn't want my son to be alarmed. As the ambulance doors closed, I heard a soft voice inside my mind:

"Do not worry, my child, for there is another."

I was bewildered by this voice coming from within my mind. I didn't try to understand the significance of the words that were spoken because too much was happening around me. I couldn't stop my body from shaking as I lay there on the stretcher. I could hear the echoing sirens as the paramedic put a warm blanket over me and took my vitals. I stared at the ceiling, feeling totally disconnected from the reality of what was going on, as though in a dream, but deep down, I knew that I wasn't alone; I was at peace.

"I'm sorry, Mrs. Harvey, you had a miscarriage. There is nothing that could have prevented this," said the attending physician in a most compassionate way.

"We're going to get you ready for a D&C." I knew what he meant because of my nursing background. They were going to dilate my cervix and scrape the walls of my uterus with a curette, a surgical tool used in that procedure. "You will be going up to the operating room shortly," continued the doctor as he left the room.

I couldn't grasp the reality of what was said. I just lay there as though lost in a fog. Then, suddenly out of nowhere, I saw Dr. Burcoletti, my gynecologist, walking towards me.

"How are you doing, Carmen," said Dr. Burcoletti as he leaned over to talk to me. "Before we send you for a D&C, I am going to send you for an ultrasound."

It was a blessing from God that Dr. Burcoletti was on call that day. The ultrasound revealed that there was another baby, and there she was in utero with her two fists in the air.

"She's a fighter!" said Peter rushing into the room. He gently kissed me on the forehead as he lay his hand on my belly. He was relieved that I was well and so elated to hear that our daughter was out of danger. Peter had left work in a hurry when he received the call from my parents. He was beside himself with worry, but Dr. Burcoletti put him at ease when he explained the situation and revealed the result of the ultrasound.

"Peter, I'm so happy you're here. I can't believe it; it's a miracle!" I said, beaming with joy.

I was pregnant with two fraternal twins. The doctor said we would have lost both if I had not hemorrhaged—in other words, the loss of one had saved the other! After I hemorrhaged, my cervix had miraculously closed itself. We would have lost them both with the D&C. It was a miracle!

Peter and I had no idea we were expecting twins, but God knew! Suddenly I remembered the words spoken to me in the ambulance and realized that it was God. I had felt His presence and peace within me. He was there with me in that ambulance, comforting and reassuring me that all would be well. God kept His promise from the dream of long ago. I was not alone—He would always be with me.

Katherine Dona Harvey (aka KD Harvey) was born May 15, 1992, at 13:02, weighing seven pounds, eleven ounces. She was a beautiful, bouncing baby girl with reddish hair. Katherine was our miracle from God! My dad was so happy to see the reddish hair because of our Irish heritage. Grandma Bernard came to visit us in the hospital with my parents. Tears welled in her eyes as she looked at Katherine. I knew why. Grandma had also suffered the loss of a twin child. She had carried both to full term; however her little girl was stillborn. Her son, my uncle, had survived. She did not have to say anything to me; we understood each other's pain.

I was so grateful to God that one twin had survived, yet would grieve the loss of the other.

Years later, we gave our unborn daughter the name Cessna. I chose that name because my husband enjoyed flying and it was the name of his favorite airplane.

"Peter, I wish Cessna would have lived. Do you often think about how it would have been different, especially for KD to have a sister, for us as a family?" I said, choking back tears.

"Carmen, I try not to focus on what we have lost, but on the blessings that are in front of us," said Peter as he reached for my hand. I understood what he meant, but it's normal for a mother to miss a child that she never held. Now and then, I think of her, but I know that she is in heaven, which brings me much comfort.

I have seen Cessna several times, once in a dream as a child of five and in a vision in her early teens. In that vision, she was sitting on the bleachers, outside, watching Denis, my brother playing football. He looked so content and at peace, but he seemed so different. He appeared more youthful, and a bright light emanated from his face. I was puzzled, so I asked the Holy Spirit why he looked so young and shone so bright.

"Carmen, in heaven, you continue to learn the Word," said the Holy Spirit. "As you grow in the knowledge of God, His glory radiates within and through you at a greater intensity."

I later shared this vision from God with my parents, and it greatly encouraged them to know about their son and how happy he was.

CHOKING ON A PIECE OF CARPET
-January 1992-

"Peter, the carpet downstairs in the rec room needs to be changed; it's coming apart in some areas," I said to my husband as he played with the children in the living room.

"Yes, I noticed last week that the foam under the carpet is disintegrating," replied Peter.

"Sweetheart, I am worried because it could be a choking hazard for the children."

"Yes, I agree." Peter replied. "I'm going to remove the carpet and look for some tiles this weekend."

"That would be great," I said with a sigh of relief as I set the table for dinner.

The following day, KD, who was now eight months old, was crawling on the carpet downstairs and accidentally swallowed a piece of black foam from the side of the carpet. The foam lodged itself in her trachea and immediately blocked her airway. She collapsed on the floor in front of me as her pale white skin turned bluish. She was not breathing!

I ran and picked up her limp body in my arms. She was like a ragged doll. My nursing instincts took over. I immediately started the Heimlich maneuver. While opening her mouth, I saw a black piece of foam and removed it. I ran up the stairs with KD in my arms and called 911. When the paramedics arrived, KD was no longer in distress. The paramedics who assessed her told me that she would be fine. I felt reassured but remained shaken from the incident; my entire body felt drained of all its energy. When the paramedics left the house, I plopped onto the floor and sobbed uncontrollably. I was so angry with myself about the carpet.

I put KD in her crib for an afternoon nap a few hours later. I was in the kitchen when suddenly I had an unsettled feeling inside to check in on her. It was the same feeling that I had experienced long ago when I lost my brother. Without hesitation, I quickly went into her room and realized that she was choking. I opened her mouth and removed another little piece of foam that she had regurgitated.

When Peter came home, I ran into his arms and cried, "Our daughter could have died today because of that stupid carpet."

"I'm so sorry that happened. Are you okay? How's KD?" worriedly said Peter as he quickly removed his boots to go see the children. "That carpet is gone tonight!"

God was looking after our little one that day; He was there the whole time. I am so thankful that I listened to the "inner prompting" from the Holy Spirit, that stirring from within telling me that something was not quite right.

THE GREEN LIGHT
-Summer 1993-

It was another busy day as I hurriedly dressed our two children for their doctor's appointments. The office was at the corner of a busy street downtown. I parked the car a few blocks away since there was no available parking space nearby. I decided to leave the stroller in the car.

Upon leaving the doctor's office, we walked to the corner of a busy intersection. The crossing light was red. John was standing right beside me, holding my hand, while KD had her head nestled against my left shoulder. As we waited for the light to turn green, I heard a soft whispering voice within my mind:

"Do not cross the road on the green light. A car will be turning the corner. The driver will be looking towards the back and will not see you. You will be hit."

I continued to wait, struggling between the voice that I heard and my own mind wanting to cross. The light turned green, and I didn't move. *Should I cross, or shouldn't I?* I thought to myself. *This is crazy!* I stood there for probably 10 seconds or more, but it felt like forever. So, I decided to take one step forward. As I did, a taxi turned the corner to the left of us. The driver drove at a faster-than-usual speed and had his head turned towards the back. We were but a foot away from being hit. He had not seen us! Those seconds of hesitation saved our lives. It was also a blessing that I had left the stroller in the car because that one step forward would have been disastrous.

The Holy Spirit protected us that day. My hesitation or stubbornness in not listening and trusting Him could have cost us our lives. It was difficult to fully grasp that I heard an actual voice speaking to me within my mind. It was not coming from me—from my intellect. I began to question myself because it was surreal; it was unexplainable!

In the Old Testament, Samuel heard the audible voice of God calling him three times **(1 Samuel 3:1-10)**. When God called him, he did not recognize His voice because it was unfamiliar to him.

Samuel was serving the Lord under Eli. He knew of God but had never heard His voice. I could relate to that passage of scripture; I knew about God but had to learn to recognize the whispering voice of His Spirit. It was not familiar to me. It would take several more encounters for me to know His voice and become more sensitive to His leading. When the Holy Spirit spoke to me as a soft whisper in my mind, I was never afraid. I might have doubted the source, but there was always a peace within me.

CHAPTER 17

A MESSAGE IN SONG

A GLIMPSE OF MY CALLING

I started singing more of my original songs in church and whenever we had gatherings at the house. Because I enjoyed teaching and singing, the Pastor asked me to help with Sunday school.

"Father Abraham had many sons, many sons had Father Abraham," I melodiously sang as the children stomped their feet and clapped their hands.

The children loved the music and enjoyed accompanying me with the rhythm sticks and tambourines. Teaching Sunday School worked out well since John and KD were both in my class, and I enjoyed doing arts and crafts and reading stories from the Bible.

One day, the Pastor asked if I could sing a song for the following Sunday's service. I was so excited! That week words out of nowhere began to pour into my mind as I wrote and composed a song called: "Who Are You to Judge Me Saith the Lord." I was thirty-one years old when I wrote that song.

Sunday came, and off I went to the front to sing. As I strummed my guitar, I sang confidently with enthusiasm. A dead silence fell upon the room as I returned to my seat. All I could hear was the pounding of my heart against my chest as I waited for the Pastor to speak. He just stood there at the podium like a statue, as though frozen in time!

What is going on? I thought to myself as I sat down beside my husband. *Please, someone, say something! Why is it so silent?* It was so quiet that you could have heard a pin drop. After several minutes, the Pastor finally uttered a few words to the congregants, and I was finally able to breathe.

The Pastor never asked me to sing in church, and he never explained to me the reason why.

I never sang that song again! It was for that specific time and place. This was the song:

"WHO ARE YOU TO JUDGE ME"

Who are you to judge me saith the Lord?
Who are you to judge me saith the Lord?
Have you gone so far away from Me?
You can't see the light, you can't see the light

You come to My Church saith the Lord
You say that you are one of Mine
But you don't pray to Me
I see through you, I cry for you
Love on another as I have loved you
Break those walls, get closer to Me
Praise My name

Who are you to judge me saith the Lord?
Who are you to judge my people now?

Have you gone so far away from Me?
You can't see the light
You can't see the light
Spirit of Saul I'll cut you down
Spirit of Jezebel I'll cast you to the sea,
I'll cast you to the sea
Deceive not My people,
Take care of My sheep
Love one another as I have loved you
Break those walls, get closer to Me
Praise My name

The day of judgment will draw near
The Book will be opened, and you will see
The wrong that you've done to My sheep
And I will say…… I don't know you

Copyright 1993, CC Harvey Music.

It was not the last time that God would use me to deliver messages in song. When the Holy Spirit gave me the lyrics for that song, I had no idea what the church was going through at the time and didn't know what a Jezebel Spirit or what a Spirit of Saul was. Several years later, someone confided in me that the Church had problems within the leadership and between some of its congregants. Many would succumb to spiritual abuse and eventually leave the Church.

Unbeknown to me, the Holy Spirit had given me a message of conviction for the Church. Now, had I known the song's intent, I don't think I could have delivered the message with the same level of confidence. I believe that God kept me from that knowledge for me to accomplish His work.

God prepares and equips every Believer for Kingdom purpose, to serve Him where we are in our ordinary lives. We are the light of Christ to the world, bringing glory to God through loving and serving those around us.

"For we are God's handiwork, created in Christ Jesus to do good works, which God prepared in advance for us to do." (Ephesians 2:10, NIV)

I started to realize that the guitar given by my father years ago was not only a seed planted by God to help me through the trials but also prepare me for Kingdom purpose. This experience was but a glimpse of my calling.

CHAPTER 18

THE GIRL IN THE PICTURE FRAME

In 1994, two years after KD was born, we visited my husband's parents in Toronto, Ontario. One afternoon while chatting with his parents in the living room, I noticed a photo of a little girl in a silver-white frame on an old French-style hall table. Something intrigued me about it. I got up to have a closer look and couldn't believe my eyes. The little girl in the photo was probably around four or five years old, had curly blond hair, rosy cheeks, blue eyes, and had a light blue dress. She looked familiar to me. Suddenly I understood why. She had a strong resemblance to the little girl in the dream I had before the miscarriage—the one who held my brother's hand.

"Dona, who is the little girl in this picture?" I said with enthusiasm as I held the frame in my hand. "Is it a relative?"

"No, my dear, that is a photo that was taken of me when I was five years old," said Dona sipping her tea in a most refined manner.

"That photo looks identical to the little girl I dreamed about, our daughter!" I whispered to Peter as I sat down beside him.

I knew that Dona did not want to discuss the matter further by the silence in the room, but the picture confirmed that our daughter in heaven looked like Grandma Harvey.

CHAPTER 19

THE LEMON

-Summer of 1995-

My husband arrived home one day with an old burgundy van that he purchased at a great price from one of our neighbours. He didn't consult me beforehand but instead decided to surprise me.

"Come outside, Carmen," said Peter, his eyes gleaming with excitement. "I have something to show you!"

There was no way to hide my disappointment when I saw the van because I'm like an open book.

"Why didn't you ask me before buying this? You knew that I didn't want another burgundy van."

I wasn't impressed! It was futile for me to continue the conversation because it was a done deal, and my husband did buy it with good intentions in mind. However, that van turned out to be a real lemon; from failing brakes to headlights not working, and more. It gave us so much trouble!

On a warm summer day, while driving back home, I approached an intersection where the light had just turned green. I was about half a mile from home.

"Turn left at the mall," said a voice inside my mind. I briefly hesitated because I wanted to get home. "Turn left, now!" insisted the voice in a much harsher tone. I had heard that familiar voice before, it had saved our lives. There was no time for self-doubt; I immediately turned left and went to park the van. As I turned the engine off, the whole front axle fell with a loud thud onto the pavement. It was difficult for me to take in what had just happened, so I just sat there behind the wheel, unable to move or say anything—I was in shock. From the passenger side, I could see an older man with an astonished look on his face. He had seen the axle fall.

"Are you alright?" said the man as he walked towards the vehicle. "You're lucky you weren't driving."

"I'm fine, a little shaken right now, but I'm okay!"

That incident was the last straw for me. A week later we bought another van, and it wasn't burgundy!

I was so grateful to have listened to the voice without too much hesitation this time. By God's grace, the Holy Spirit had protected me from imminent danger.

CHAPTER 20

END TIME DREAM

My first "end time" dream was in 1998. I was thirty-five years old. In the first part of the dream, I saw a dragon-like beast in chains restlessly thrashing from side to side. I wanted to look at the face of the beast, but God said that it was not important for me to see but to know that the time was drawing near.

In the second part of the dream, I saw a woman on her knees in an open field, frantically clinging to three young children. Their eyes were full of fear as a man in a black suit approached them. He had a wild look in his eyes as he held on to what appeared to be a hand-held scanner, like those seen in grocery stores, but smaller and narrower.

"Take the mark, and your children will never know hunger," said the man void of all emotions.

"No, no, never!" relentlessly yelled the woman. I could see the anguish on her face as she firmly held on to the children.

In the third part of the dream, I saw a middle-aged woman holding on to a chain-link fence with both hands, stoically staring ahead. She stood there in a statuesque pose, undisturbed by the wind blowing her brown wavy hair into her face. I sensed loneliness but knew that this woman had great strength and was a force to be reckoned with. She was a survivor, a warrior! I saw mass apocalyptic destruction through the fence: the surface of the ground and everything upon it was darkened like coal, as though hit by intense heat. The stench of death was everywhere.

I was so deeply troubled by this dream that I wrote my first end-time song.

"LEAD ME ON"

I had a dream of a woman kneeling to the ground,
clinging desperately to her child
There was a man standing with a wild look in his eyes,
wanting to give her the mark of the beast
She cried, "No, no, no"
"No, no, no"

It was written in God's word that this would come one day

Lead me on, lead me on
Lead me on, to tell the world
To tell the world

I had a dream of a beast in a cave
Bound with chains, he was thrashing to and fro
God said the beast was restless
"Be prepared for I am coming"

Lead me on, lead me on
Lead me on, to tell the world
To tell the world

I had a dream of a woman looking through an iron fence
There was fire and destruction everywhere
There was smoke, and the sky was red
People were dying everywhere

It was written in God's word that this would come one day

Lead me on, lead me on
Lead me on, to tell the world
To tell the world

Copyright 1998, CC Harvey Music.

It says in God's Word that He speaks and reveals much to us through dreams.

"In the last days, God says, I will pour out my Spirit on all people. Your sons and daughters will prophesy, your young men will see visions, your old men will dream dreams." (Acts 2:17, NIV)

"He speaks in dreams, in visions of the night, when deep sleep falls on people as they lie in their beds. He whispers in their ears and terrifies them with warnings. He makes them turn from doing wrong; he keeps them from pride. He protects them from the grave, from crossing over the river of death." (Job 33:15-18, NLT)

This end-time dream was to be the first of many other dreams that I would receive and sing about later in my life.

CHAPTER 21

FIBRO MONSTER

-1995-2005-

"I don't know what's wrong with me; I feel so tired all the time," I said to Peter one evening as I slumped beside him on the couch. I was not one to complain, but my whole body ached all over, and I didn't have any energy at all; I was tired all the time!

During the mid-'90s, our family physician had ordered countless blood work and tests to find the root cause of the pain. He wanted to make sure that it wasn't Lupus Erythematosus or Multiple Sclerosis. I also underwent nerve conduction tests because of the numbness in my extremities, but the results were all negative. On one occasion, the blood work had revealed a slightly positive ANA (antinuclear antibody test). This test would have confirmed the presence of an autoimmune disease; unfortunately, the repeat blood work came back negative. Since nothing was ever conclusive, the doctor would repeatedly tell me that the pain I was experiencing was psychosomatic, meaning the pain was coming from my mind. Therefore, the doctor suggested that I see a psychiatrist, which I politely declined. It was difficult to fathom that my mind caused the pain because it was real and debilitating; It upset me!

In the late '90s, I finally received a diagnosis. A Rheumatologist in Southern Ontario tested me for all eighteen trigger points (AKA tender points) associated with a disorder called fibromyalgia. For this test, the doctor pressed firmly on eighteen specific areas of my body to see if it would cause me to have pain, and it did: waves of it pulsating through my body. That test confirmed that I had fibromyalgia.

Fibromyalgia is a very complex disease that still baffles the medical profession. In the '90s, many scientists believed that the pain associated with fibromyalgia was due to trauma in a person's life that altered their brain's biochemistry. However, in 2022, scientists found evidence through PET scans that people with fibromyalgia had widespread inflammation across their brains. Was my pain derived from past traumas? Possibly, but I believe it was a bit of both. I was still living with the emotional wounds of what happened to me as a child, but I also think there could have been inflammation in my brain because it made sense. Inflammation within my brain would cause havoc with my body's central nervous system and cause my nerve cells to overreact. Signalling problems would occur, and as a result, I would experience muscle pain throughout my body. That made sense to me!

"Unfortunately, people with fibromyalgia are still sometimes told it's all in their heads. The inflammatory evidence shows that's half true—the answer might lie in patient's brains, but not in their imagination."
—Benjamin Abraham, MD (Expert in pain management)

This Fibro-Monster affected my lower back, the area where I had sustained my nursing injury. Because of that, I would have difficulty walking at times. It didn't care! My cane was my constant companion during those times. One day, my mother came unexpectedly to the house and was shocked to see me in such a state. She was clueless about the severity of my condition. No one knew the depth of what I was living with because I didn't want anyone to see me like that.

I had difficulties with my memory (AKA brain fog) which was common with fibromyalgia. One day while shopping with my daughter, I held up a shirt and said, "Hey KD, what do you think of these pants?" A lady passed by and gave us a funny look. I realized what I had said and started laughing. It became the norm for me to mix up my words or have difficulty in finding words to complete sentences. In those moments, I would laugh at myself. Laughter was the best therapy!

It was socially awkward for me to be around big crowds because I could not focus on any conversation. Apart from family, our social life was non-existent. I had stopped going to church since standing and sitting for extended periods completely exhausted me and caused too much pain.

My father was concerned and decided to call Dr. Tony, a friend and hunting partner. I was to see him in October at their hunting camp. Dr. Tony was a psychiatrist who had immigrated from England. He was an expert in fibromyalgia and had done extensive research in the field while treating many of the veterans returning from the Vietnam war.

The day we met, I had difficulties grasping everything he said because of his accent. Still, it was a great relief for me to speak to a professional who understood the pain that I was experiencing.

"Carmen, the pain that you are experiencing is real, but you need to learn to manage it," said Dr. Tony as he took notes.

He was right; when you live with a lot of pain, every minor stressor in your life becomes a mountain—sometimes a volcano ready to erupt.

I had a tough time coping with the little things that came my way; it would cause me to lack patience, have anxiety and be irritable.

"I'm going to prescribe an antidepressant to help control the pain," said Dr. Tony. "It will also lessen the anxiety that you have been experiencing."

I hated being on an antidepressant; I gained a lot of weight and felt this numbness in my brain, this disconnect with the world around me, but it did reduce the intensity of the pain.

During the ten years that I lived with this illness, my husband was always so supportive and had faith that I would be well again.

"Carmen, you're going to be okay. It's going to get better," said Peter every morning before going to work. Even when I was grumpy and miserable, he was loving and patient with me. It was difficult for him to see me suffer, but he believed that someday I would get better. He even posted a little note on our fridge: "Tomorrow is another day!"

Peter did most of the outdoor sporting activities with the children during this time since I had too much pain and was afraid to fall and hurt myself.

"Mom, I don't want to go to school today. I want to stay home and help you," said KD as she gently snuggled up to me on the couch. She was determined to stay home, and I didn't have the energy to argue. Deep down, I wanted her to stay home because I was having such a rough day. KD was nine years old and loved to draw. That day, as I lay on the couch resting, she drew a beautiful picture of me smiling. At the top of it, she wrote: "Get better, Mommy, I love you."

Living with this disorder was difficult for me. I no longer recognized the woman that I saw in the mirror. I grieved the loss of who I used to be. I had to learn to accept my limitations, redefine and love myself.

Music was essential for me; I would play guitar and sing several hours a day. It soothed my soul and helped me to cope with the pain. It drew me closer to God as I poured my heart to Him. Music was a place of refuge for me; it was my time with God. It gave me so much joy and peace.

In the latter years of living with fibromyalgia, I developed a very rare mental disorder called cyclothymia which would cause me to have weeks of high energy followed by weeks of low energy. I never had extreme mood swings like some people experience with this disorder. To be honest, cyclothymia was a blessing in disguise. When I had those weeks of high energy, they enabled me to do things despite the pain. By the grace of God, I was able to be involved with projects such as "Airwaves" and eventually release my first album.

CHAPTER 22

"AIRWAVES"

-1997-

"Carmen, can you do some announcements for us?" said the General Manager of CHIM FM 102.3. CHIM was Canada's first non-commercial Christian radio station broadcasting from Timmins, Ontario.

I became a casual announcer and concert promoter for CHIM in 1997. During that time, a friend and I started "Northern Opry," a promotion company for Canadian Christian Artists. We decided to put together a compilation CD (a compact disc) that would feature artists from various genres of Christian music, and organize a concert for CHIM at the same time as the release of the album. "Airwaves - His World, His Music" was the chosen name for the compilation and upcoming concert.

Because Orville and I had a strong interest in learning more about the music industry, we arranged a meeting with Mary Bailey in Kirkland Lake.

Mary Bailey's office was impressive, with mahogany bookcases and walls adorned with many awards. It was a little intimidating for me, but she had a way of making you feel right at home. As she sat behind her desk, she offered us something to drink, and kindly gestured for us to sit. She talked at great lengths about the music business, and it was quite evident that she had experienced a lot in her career. Mary Bailey had received a recording contract with RCA Victor (Canada) in the mid-'70s and released several singles that earned her national airplay. Later, she would become Shania Twain's manager and play an integral role in launching her career. Although she shared with us the ups and downs of the music business, there was one piece of advice that she gave me that I would never forget:

"Carmen, everything that you do, do it to the best of your ability because it is a reflection of who you are."

Within a month, we had found nine artists to be featured on the album and hired a local musician to record and produce the songs. Orville turned his garage into a makeshift studio. It wasn't fancy, but it worked. The entire project was finished within four months and recorded on an old analog reel-to-reel tape recorder; yes, we still used analog back then!

It was a hectic time for me as I scheduled the artists for their recording sessions and organized all the practices. Working with different artists with their own expectations was challenging, but I realized that I couldn't please everyone. We had schedules to maintain and a concert that was quickly approaching. I had to learn to be assertive.

There were times when I got on my knees and cried out to God:

"Lord, I don't know if I have the strength to do this? Please help me."

I lacked so much confidence in myself. It wasn't easy to be in a leadership position because everyone looked up to me and depended on me. Everyone was unaware that I suffered from fibromyalgia. The stress of it all started affecting me significantly, creating many anxieties within me. I was beginning to show signs of burnout.

It was also hard for me because I had a five-year-old daughter at home who wanted my attention. Every time I got on the phone, KD would grab me by the leg or tug at my shirt and start whining:

"Mommy get off the phone! Mommy!"

I kept trying to do things on my own strength rather than trusting the Holy Spirit. In those moments of great discouragement, I had to learn to surrender and be led by Him. It wasn't easy, but I found that the Holy Spirit would empower me and give me the confidence to move forward when I took the time to pray. In those times, I felt that I wasn't alone.

I enjoyed every minute of working on this project because I found purpose in knowing that I was doing something for the Kingdom. It made me feel good about myself since I had lost so much of who I was because of fibromyalgia.

A promotional campaign for the concert was created and well received by the media. In the evening of June 27th, 1992, a few hours before the concert, all the artists gathered backstage. There were eleven of us, including the master of ceremonies and makeup artist. We prayed together and shared our thoughts. We were all excited yet nervous at the same time.

Because of a successful marketing campaign, we managed to sell three-hundred tickets. We were performing to a packed house.

The concert was a resounding success. We received two standing ovations and great local press coverage. Many were blessed that evening and hearts stirred by the presence of the Holy Spirit. That event turned out to be one of the biggest Christian concerts ever held in Timmins, Ontario.

After "Airwaves," we were invited to perform at "Canada Day" and other venues. It was an amazing time of sharing God's love through music.

"Airwaves" was such a blessing, but unfortunately, the stress of doing a project of that magnitude in such a brief period took its toll on me physically and worsened my condition; therefore, I had to retreat from the music scene to take care of myself. "Northern Opry" was a great idea but was short-lived.

I have learned over the years that remarkable things happen when you let God lead the way. The journey is not always easy. There are times of incredible frustration and moments of discouragement, but one thing is for certain: God is always there to uplift and empower us.

> **"For I can do everything through Christ, who gives me strength" (Philippians 4:13, NLT)**

CHAPTER 23

TUNED IN TO GOD'S CHANNEL

DANGLING UPSIDE DOWN
-Fall of 1999-

"Your daughter is outside, dangling upside down," said a whispering voice in my mind as I was watching television downstairs. It was early evening, and KD, now seven years old, was playing outside in the snow. I tried to ignore the voice but heard again, "Your daughter is outside, dangling upside down."

I was a bit upset since I didn't want to be disturbed—I was selfish and wanted some time to myself. Mothers need that sometimes. Nevertheless, I knew that it was the Holy Spirit, and I couldn't avoid Him. I abruptly stomped up the stairs, opened the sliding glass door to the back deck, and sure enough, there was my daughter, dangling upside down. KD had jumped off the deck, and the lace of her boot had caught itself in the barbecue's side table. She was flaring her arms, unable to detach herself. To the rescue, I went!

It amazes me that God is concerned about every little aspect of our lives, even a child dangling upside down! We serve a God who knows everything about us, even the number of hairs on our heads **(Luke 12:7)**. He cares about all the little details of our lives; we are so precious to Him. It is so important to learn to recognize the voice of the Holy Spirit, and the many ways He communicates with us. He speaks to us through God's Word, inner promptings, people, visions, dreams, and through God's creation. As we spend more time with God in prayer and His Word, we become more sensitive to the presence of the Holy Spirit in our life; we become tuned in to God's channel!

GOD LET ME BE OKAY
-July 2000-

The sun shone brightly through streaks of puffy clouds adorning a clear blue sky. We decided to take advantage of this beautiful day and go for a family bike ride on one of the nature trails around Northern College in South Porcupine. John, now ten years old, enjoyed speeding ahead of us. We arrived at a fork in the road. I decided to turn right with KD and go home, while my husband turned left to go and catch up to John. After we parted, I began to regret the decision that I had made. I felt a restlessness within me. I knew something was wrong! There was an urgency within me to ride as fast as possible on another path that would intercept them. So, I did.

I arrived at the location where the path intersected with the road they were on. As I looked up, I saw John lying on his back, halfway down the hill. My husband was not yet in sight. I could feel my heart fiercely beating in my chest as I frantically rushed to his side.

"God, let me be okay! God, let me be okay!" yelled John as he looked under his shorts. A torn chunk of skin exposed a pulsating artery. John needed emergency care. My head started spinning as I imagined the worst.

"It's okay, John, Mommy's here!" I said as Peter got off his bike and ran towards us.

A man walking his dog approached us and offered to help. His presence gave us much comfort while my husband left to get help. That man was indeed an angel sent by God.

The ambulance arrived and took John to the hospital, where he received deep stitches and seven surface stitches to an L-shape laceration.

John later explained that his front wheel had caught a wooden stump as he was speeding down the hill. He was thrown off his bike into the bush beside the trail. A wooden twig sticking out of the ground had pierced his left inner thigh missing an artery.

God was there on that hill listening to the cries of my son. He was not alone! I believe that the Holy Spirit prompted not only me but that man walking his dog to be there for John.

CHAPTER 24

MY FIRST ALBUM RELEASE

-Fall 2000-

During the three years after "Airwaves," I wrote and composed over twenty country songs. Since I enjoyed country music so much, I decided to release a mini-album or CD (compact disc) of five of my songs. Easier said than done. First and foremost, I needed to find a producer who understood my music and the direction I wanted to take. Secondly, I didn't have six thousand dollars to pay for the recording and production of this album. I needed to find a way to make money to pay for it all.

One day, out of nowhere came this incredible idea. Every Friday and Saturday, I would attend various local yard sales to find antiques and collectibles to sell online. This endeavour proved to be quite a success.

On one of those Saturdays, I found a medium-sized box tucked in the corner of someone's kitchen. To my surprise, the box was full of 1980s Gem Barbie clothes, in mint condition, still in their boxes. Every single one of those outfits sold for five hundred dollars apiece online. I had over twelve of them! That find paid for the album!

In honor of Gramma Cécile, I decided at that time to change my name to CC Harvey (Carmen Cécile Harvey). It would become my adopted stage name.

Releasing this album was difficult because I didn't know how Believers that knew me as a gospel singer would respond. I don't know why I felt like that; they were good wholesome Country songs. Unfortunately, later in the summer, while at a yard sale, I would have a terrible encounter with a woman who called herself a Christian.

"Are you still singing?" she said while trying to avoid eye contact.

"Yes, I am," I cautiously replied, not knowing where the conversation was going." I just released a country album."

"Is it gospel music?"

"No, it's a country album," I joyfully said as I glanced at some of the items on the table in front of me.

"Are you backslidden?"

I felt my face turn red as I just stood there in disbelief. *Did she just say that to me?* I thought to myself. According to the Google dictionary, backslidden means to relapse into bad ways or errors. To further make her point, she started quoting scriptures from the Bible. I was taken aback and hurt by her words. *You don't know me,*

I thought to myself. *You don't know my heart. Why are you judging me?* I took a deep breath, smiled and with my head up high confidently walked away, fully aware that I was dealing with a spirit of religion. I later realized that the enemy had attacked me through this woman. He tried to discourage me and make me believe that I was not a Believer. *Why? Because I sang country songs? How ridiculous was that!* I said to myself. I was not going to let that water into my boat; I wasn't going to accept those lies from the enemy.

The album "Straight from Your Heart" was written and composed through the pain of living with fibromyalgia and cyclothymia. I worked on this project with Rick Ash, a well-known Christian Producer, and many great industry musicians. It was an album with many quirky love songs like "Ocean Potion" and "Straight from Your Heart." The single release "Money Flies Out—Love Strikes Out" was about a woman who blamed her shopping sprees on her husband. It was a fun song with a very catchy tune. I wrote this song because I enjoyed shopping, and knew that many people would relate to it. "Baby Blue Eyes" was written for my daughter KD. The song was about a mother's love for her daughter.

"As long as the stars shine in the sky, as long as the moon smiles from up high. That's how long my love will be for you. I'm not going anywhere soon cause I'm looking after you. You're my baby blue eyes," I ardently sang in front of a large crowd at my release party. There was not one dry-eyed person in the whole room. It was voted that evening as one of the best songs on the album.

A dozen radio stations across Canada played my music. It was exciting when I heard one of my songs playing on our local country radio station for the very first time while driving in my car. I felt giddy like a child.

I received invitations to perform at various concerts in the community, including my daughter's grade two class at Frank P. Krznaric Whitney Public School in Porcupine, Ontario. I had such an amazing time with the children, singing and teaching them about music. It was priceless to see the excitement on their little faces, especially when I gave them each a CD.

When I left the school during recess, I found myself surrounded by children wanting an autograph. It was a very heartwarming experience for me! The following week, several children came to our door for an autograph. I will never forget those precious moments and how blessed I was to have put this album together by the grace of God.

However, my musical journey would end abruptly due to ongoing struggles with my health.

CHAPTER 25

THE NAIL CLIPPER

-Fall 2002-

"Hey, CC! I'm singing on 100 Huntley Street tomorrow morning," enthusiastically said Laurie over the telephone. She was so excited to share the good news with me.

Laurie was a good friend and an anointed Christian Singer/Songwriter from Southern Ontario. Though she stood at four feet, eleven inches, God had graced her with a powerful set of lungs. I was excited for her and looked forward to hearing her sing.

I enjoyed watching 100 Huntley Street, a popular Christian television show. It was encouraging to listen to testimonies by other Believers, whether they were everyday people, celebrities, or famous leaders. They would also invite Christian artists to sing on their programs.

I was sitting on my knees on the floor, about six feet away from the TV set. I could feel God's presence in the room as Laurie sang, "He Leads Us On," a beautiful song of praise unto the Lord. Suddenly, a small nail clipper on the top of the television flew off and hit me on the right upper leg.

"Ouch!" I yelled.

I was stunned and felt goosebumps all over my arms. I knew right away that there was an evil spirit in the room. I was aware of this because of the many encounters I had as a child, but I had never been physically hurt by them. This time, I was unnerved. It would have taken considerable force to propel that four-inch nail clipper at me from six feet away. I immediately stood up and looked to my right because the Holy Spirit had revealed to me where the unwelcomed spirit was.

I was pretty shaken by what had just happened, but God gave me the boldness to say:

"Now I'm upset! I am a Child of God, covered with the blood of Jesus Christ. Do not mess with me! In the name of Jesus, I command you to leave this place and go to the pit of hell where you belong."

After praying a few minutes longer, I felt God's peace within and around me. The heaviness that was in the room left.

Several days later, I called my friend Laurie and told her about what had happened. Her song of praise unto the Lord had infuriated the evil spirit present in the room.

My son later informed me that he had visited a friend who liked to play occultist games. A spirit from that home had become an unwelcome guest in ours. That experience with the nail clipper made me realize, once again, that as Believers, we continuously fight against unknown principalities. I learned that we battle and defeat the enemy through praise and worship, prayer, and the acquired knowledge of God's Word.

"Be alert and of sober mind. Your enemy the devil prowls around like a roaring lion looking for someone to devour." (1 Peter 5:8, NIV)

The Holy Spirit had made known to me the whereabouts of this unwelcomed spirit and gave me the boldness and courage to take authority over it in the name of Jesus.

There is so much power in the name of Jesus! At His name, demons flee, for in Jesus there is victory!

CHAPTER 26

SAYING GOODBYE

I regret not visiting Grandma Cécile more in the last few years of her life. Since Grandma had fallen several times and broken her hip, her daughters decided it was in her best interest to live in a long-term care facility. Her bones had become fragile and brittle—they were like Cinderella's glass slipper!

It was so hard for me! I was so scared of losing another person in my life, especially Grandma! I could not bear to see her so frail. The only way for me to cope was to distance myself. I did visit her from time to time, but not nearly enough!

Grandma and I were close. There was a special bond between us. A few days before she passed away, the family gathered around her bed. By this time, Grandma had lost the ability to see and had become quite deaf. As I entered the room, Grandma lay peacefully on her right side. I gently approached her, and whispered in her left ear, "Hi, Grandma. It's me, Carmen. I'm here!" Suddenly, Grandma said in a soft, frail voice, "Carmen!" She knew I was there! Everyone in the room was surprised and wanted me to say their names out loud, but Grandma only responded to my name. I knew she had missed me, but that day she acknowledged my presence, and in so doing brought solace to my heart.

As we all stood together, we prayed and sang Grandma's favorite song, "Amazing Grace." I wanted to cry, but it was important for me to sing one last time for Grandma!

Grandma Cécile went on to meet the Lord in March of 2003, at the age of ninety-three. I miss her very much!

I wrote the following song in 2017 in memory of Grandma, a faithful servant of God.

"GOD'S ANGELS CARRIED HER"

Grandma never had too much money
All she knew was poverty
Stayed home to raise her brothers
Gave up all her dreams

Every day she'd pray
For the Lord to show the way
To true happiness and love
God's angels carried her,
and her prayers would be heard
From a servant's heart

Grandma met a man
Her dying Momma said to marry
Back then, you did as you were told

ALWAYS NEVER ALONE

Every day she'd pray
For the Lord to show the way
To true happiness and love
God's angels carried her,
and her prayers would be heard
From a servant's heart

Grandma sits in her rocking chair,
reading a Bible with trembling hands
Every now and then, she'd write a line or two
To bless us daily with God's Word
Grandma looks at me with a twinkle in her eye
Hiding a secret like a Mona Lisa smile

Every day she'd pray
For the Lord to show the way
To true happiness and love
God's angels carried her,
and her prayers would be heard
From a servant's heart
Through her children, through her children
Love found its way
Through her children, through her children
Love found its way!

Copyright 2019, CC Harvey Music.

CHAPTER 27

GOD HEARD MY CRY

-Evening of May 14, 2005-

"The LORD hears his people when they call to him for help.
He rescues them from all their troubles."
(Psalm 34:17, NLT)

"But I will restore you to health and heal your
wounds, declares the Lord."
(Jeremiah 30:17, NIV)

While taking an early evening shower, I became overwhelmed by the continuous pulsating pain in my body. I leaned forward and pressed my forehead against the shower doors as the warm water trickled down my tear-drenched face; I cried out to God from the depth of my being.

"God, I can't take this pain anymore!"

I felt alone, on the edge of a cliff ready to fall—with no one to catch me.

SET FREE
-May 15, 2005-

Our daughter was having her 13th birthday, and that year, it happened to fall on a Sunday. KD took advantage of that by asking me for a very unusual gift.

"Mom, can you come to church with me today? Please!" pleaded KD as she wrapped her arms around my neck. "It could be a birthday gift from you!" *How could I possibly say no?* I thought to myself.

"Mmmm okay, I'm going to go with you." I was hesitant because I knew that going to church would increase the pain in my body, but I wanted her to be happy; it was her birthday, after all.

During the early morning worship, the Pastor asked everyone to stand. As I began to sing and worship the Lord, I felt a gentle breeze come upon me, zigzagging through my body. From the top of my chest to the bottom of my legs. I turned and looked at KD, who was standing beside me and said:

"I think—no! I'm being healed by the mighty power of God," I exclaimed. The pain I constantly felt throughout my body was instantaneously taken away; I felt alive inside!

As we left the church, I couldn't contain my excitement.

"Pastor, I was healed by the power of God during the service. I had fibromyalgia, and I no longer have any pain!" God took it all away," I said with exuberance.

"Mmmm, is that right!" said the Pastor raising an eyebrow. Judging by the incredulous look on his face, I don't think he believed me.

Nonetheless, I was so excited when we arrived home that I insisted that Peter, KD and I go for a walk to share what happened to me.

As we walked, I began having this desire to run, so I took off and ran three whole blocks, about three hundred meters. It was enough proof for Peter that something miraculous had taken place. He was shocked and delighted all at the same time. Peter knew that I would never have had the energy to do that. He always had faith that I would get better, and I did through the healing power of a wondrous God.

KD had a gymnastics competition out of town the following weekend, and I decided to go. I never attended any of these events in the past since they would set me back physically.

"Carmen, are you feeling okay?" said Peter as he walked towards me. "Do you want to go and sit for a while?"

"Peter, I'm fine!" I replied with a big smile as I watched KD doing a backbend on the beam. "God healed me, remember?" I was now full of life, full of energy!

I have had many opportunities to share my testimony of God's healing power. I can recall one occasion when I was asked by a middle-aged woman: "Why would God heal you of fibromyalgia and not me?"

Unfortunately, I didn't have the answer to that question. I don't understand why God heals one person and not the other. Who can fully comprehend the ways of God? But I know that there are reasons for everything. One day, He will reveal all to us. The greatest miracle is that of a life transformed by the power of God. A soul saved through the precious, shed blood of His Son Jesus.

I never expected to be healed that day. I never expected anything at all! I was praising and worshiping God when I felt His Spirit come upon me. I said: "I think, no! I am being healed by the mighty power of God." I quickly responded in a non- doubting way. When I spoke the words, I heard the words, and the words became real. I believed and therefore received my healing.

I am so grateful to God for His loving mercy. God heard the cry of my heart that day in the shower and healed me. I will forever praise and worship Him—give Him all the glory.

CHAPTER 28

PURSUED BY GOD

"Where can I go from your Spirit? Where can I flee from your presence? If I go up to the heavens, you are there; if I make my bed in the depths, you are there." (Psalm 139:7-9, NIV)

In the early Spring of 2006, I rented a small retail space from "Branded Spaces," a company that had developed a mini-mall in an old, four-thousand-square-foot historical building in downtown Timmins. This concept was fantastic for entrepreneurs who wanted to try out their business without committing to a long-term lease and other overhead costs.

Since I enjoyed yard sales and selling online, I decided to open an antique store and call it: "A Moment in Time Antiques." Six months into the business, I decided to import well-crafted Peruvian jewelry at a price that people could afford and at a price that I could make a profit. It was a success! Within a week, I sold all the necklaces and realized that I had found a niche market in Timmins for fashion jewelry. Because of that, I decided to change the business name to: "On the Go Fashions Inc."

I enjoyed fashion and immersed myself twelve hours a day into my work. I developed a strong online social presence and was involved with many events within and around the city.

In 2011, I relocated the business to a five hundred-square foot storefront on Wilson Avenue in Timmins, Ontario. It had proved to be an excellent financial decision with increased foot traffic and sales. Since the company was doing well, I hired Chantal, a wonderful lady who would become a great friend and a great blessing. Chantal was a devout Catholic who loved the Lord with all her heart. She was kind-hearted and had a certain peace about her that made me envious at times. I loved God, and there was not a single day that He wasn't in my thoughts, but I didn't have that inner peace, the peace that Chantal had because God was not first in my life; the business was.

Chantal and I would have these wonderful lengthy conversations about God, and many times I would share my desire to pursue the calling that God had put upon my heart—to sing again.

"Close the store and do it!" she'd casually say.

She was truly an amazing person. She wasn't thinking about herself or the probability of losing her job if I closed the store. She genuinely wanted the best for me.

Yes, I felt God's calling, but there was a continuous battle within me. One side was drawn towards a desire for self-validation through success and money, while the other side of me yearned to be used by God.

Chantal worked hard to keep up with the weekly changes and ideas that I had for the store, and believe me, it was challenging at times for her. I had been set free from fibromyalgia, but still struggled with cyclothymia. She understood the disorder that I lived with and was always supportive. Still, there were lots of new surprises every week in the store, especially when I decided to renovate or change the entire store's layout without giving her a heads up. It must have been frustrating, but she always went with the flow.

I didn't realize it at the time, but the pressure of the business was making my condition worse. I would experience weeks of high energy, which made it difficult to slow down, followed by days where I could not function at all. It was like being on a continuous roller coaster.

Everything was about "On the Go Fashions." I was constantly searching for the newest fashions and accessories to bring in, even when I was on vacation with my husband. The store was always the main topic of conversation with everyone. It had taken over my life, permeated me through and through.

One evening, while doing the dishes, the Holy Spirit softly said to me:

"Carmen, let go of the business. You're not well; you need to take care of yourself. It doesn't matter what you do in life, you'll always be successful, but it's not necessarily where God wants you to be. You can continue your journey, but it'll take more time to bring you to where God wants you to be."

Instead of listening to the Holy Spirit, I relocated the business in the Fall of 2014.

Our new location downtown had triple the space and was quite welcoming, especially with the two tub chairs placed beside the fireplace in the main entrance. Our customers appreciated being able to rest and have a cup of tea while shopping. Our store motto was: "When you look good, you feel good!" We enjoyed helping our clients find clothes that not only made them look good but fit their lifestyle and personality. We accessorized their wardrobes with the latest in fashion jewelry and offered evening shopping for those who couldn't shop during the day—we had created the perfect shopping experience for people.

It was more than just a store; it was a place where many ladies came to pour out their hearts. It was retail therapy—but we never took advantage of that. So, for example, when someone tried on an outfit that was not quite right for them, like too tight or the wrong color, we would offer our honest opinion and try to help. Honesty was important to me, and I valued that above money; our clients appreciated that.

We grew to have an excellent reputation for outstanding customer service. Our business income tripled. Our sales never went down, even during the slow seasons. But with the growth of the store came more responsibilities and more stress.

Between 2014 to 2016, God pursued me with great intensity: at night, while at the computer, the Holy Spirit would often whisper in my left ear, "Psst, Psst! What are you doing? Read the Word!"

Instead of listening to the Holy Spirit, I would put my hand over my ear to ignore Him. My soul was in danger, and God, in His mercy, was trying to reach me.

Before going to bed, usually at one or two in the morning, I would soak in a warm bath to unwind. While lying there, I would feel an invisible shackle on my right ankle, supernaturally connecting me to the heavens. Frustrated, I would look up and say: "God, what do you want from me?"

Deep within, I knew that I needed to draw closer to Him, but the world had such a stronghold on me. I didn't know how to be still. I didn't know how to let go and let God. I knew that He would never let me go. He would pursue me, but how could I let go?

GOD GETS MY ATTENTION
-Fall 2016-

My friend Marcy met me for lunch at a quaint little café around the corner from our boutique. During lunch, she said five simple words that got my attention: "I miss the old Carmen!" When I heard those words, it was as though God was saying to me, "I miss my Carmen!"

Marcy and I had become great friends over the years, and she was like a sister to me.

"Carmen, I miss the old you. Every time we talk on the phone or get together, it's all about your business. I miss our heart-to-heart conversations," Marcy confided as I silently ate my cherry pie.

What I valued about our friendship was our openness with one another. Marcy was right; everything about me was business.

Meeting my best friend that day was a "wake-up call." It was a confirmation within my soul that things needed to change in my life—and fast. I was physically, emotionally, and spiritually drowning. God had used Marcy as a vessel that day to speak to my heart, to get my attention.

I have asked for God's forgiveness for not listening and grieving the Holy Spirit. I want to be careful not to do so because He has always been there, guiding and protecting me along the way. He knows what is best for me!

Years later, I wrote a song called: "Because You Love Me" as a constant reminder of God's grace and love. A reminder to never let myself stray away from that closeness that I have with Him.

God cares deeply for His children, and He will move heaven and earth to bring us back to Him. He never gives up on us. We are so special to Him.

"BECAUSE YOU LOVE ME"

I knew you as a child
Spoke to you every day,
but somewhere along the way, I went astray

Why do I deserve Your Grace?
When there is so much darkness in my heart
Because You love me

You died for me, to set me free
Tooooooo... set me free
Tooooooo... set me
free Because You love me

There is nowhere for me to hide
You are always by my side
You oversee my life, You pursue me

Why do I deserve Your Grace?
When there is so much darkness in my heart
Because You love me
You died for me, to set me free

Copyright 2012, CC Harvey Music.

PART II

The Call

CHAPTER 29

INFILLING POWER OF THE HOLY SPIRIT

NEVER THE SAME
-Friday, January 9, 2016-

I arrived home, exhausted from yet another busy day at the store, but I had previously agreed to meet my aunts at a local church at 7:00 p.m. A Prophet had been invited to minister there for the weekend.

The ministry of the Prophet is still very much alive and needed today. It is one of the five-fold ministries of leadership that Jesus gave the Church. Prophets equip God's people for works of service and build up the body of Christ **(Ephesians 4:11-12)**. Through the Holy Spirit, they reveal the mind and heart of God.

I had no idea what to expect that evening, but what took place would forever change me.

I arrived late at the Church; over one hundred people were already there. My mother's youngest sister, Aunt Marie-Anne, had kept an empty chair for me, two seats from the aisle mid-way to the front. As the music began, everyone stood to praise and worship the Lord. Halfway through the song, I heard the soft voice of the Holy Spirit telling me to kneel. I looked to my right, looked to my left, worried about what others would say—but I knew His voice and immediately went down on my knees to worship God.

The Prophet sat in the front with his head turned away from the congregation and did not see me kneel. When the music ended, he turned around and started speaking, then suddenly stopped, looked in my direction, and pointed his finger at me.

"You!" he said.

I froze. *Was the Prophet speaking to me?*

"Yes, you!" he replied. "Do you think He's forgotten you?" As he walked towards me, my eyes began to well up with tears. *How could he possibly know what was on my heart? My desire to serve God,* I thought to myself. I was bewildered, trying to make sense of it all. I was the only one singled out in the room, and because of that, I was a bit shaken and didn't pay much attention to what he was saying to me. I only remember hearing the word "prophetic." He then gestured for me to follow him to the front.

The Prophet looked at me and, pointing his finger, said, "You have been so misunderstood." At that very moment, God's glory came upon me. Immersed in this indescribable bubble of peace, I fell backward onto the floor. There was no one behind to catch me, yet I was unhurt. I was on the floor for three hours, but it didn't feel that long at all! I can recall hearing the Prophet say, "Get used to it."

Months later, I would understand the significance of those spoken words; I would experience God's presence and glory time and time again.

As I lay on the floor, I turned my head, opened my eyes, and saw my Aunt Marie-Anne sitting beside me, holding her knee. I automatically sat up, wanting to pray, lay hands on her, but the Holy Spirit said to me gently but sternly, "It's not about her—it's about you," and right back down I went.

There was such an overwhelming joy inside me that I began to laugh. I could also hear others laughing in the room. It was a "Holy Laughter." The intensity of His presence caused me to groan at times. It came from the depth of my belly. It isn't easy to explain. It was gloriously intense! Enveloped in this "cool, peppermint sensation," I began a conversation with God in my mind. *God, can I stand up now?* I was beginning to be restless because I didn't know how to be still, even in His presence. In utter amazement, I heard God's audible voice! It wasn't a whisper; it wasn't a thought in my mind—it was a real voice. He casually said to me, in a soft, mid-tone range,

"Carmen, if you stand up, you'll go right back down." God had called me by my name!

I defiantly stood up, and He knew that I would. But, of course, He is God! But why would I do that? What I was experiencing was real, but that part of my mind still connected to the world had difficulties being still—I needed to surrender and let Him do His work within me, but I was battling. The Prophet, who was about twelve feet away from me, turned around and said, "You!" Once again, I didn't dare move. I just stood there!

"God is not done with you yet!"

"I know; He just told me," I quickly interjected, and right back down I went.

As I gradually surrendered and stopped fighting God, the fullness of His peace, His love, His glory began to pour unto me. It was electrifying. I was experiencing God's tangible glory—the power of the Holy Spirit. The same God who had spoken to me through a dream when I was ten years old had now revealed himself to me in such an intimate way—I would never be the same.

Later, as I stood up and walked back to my seat, Sally, a lady who knew me from "Airwaves," hastily approached me.

"Carmen, it's about the music, isn't it?" she asked inquisitively. I don't blame her for being curious. I was three hours on that floor, and people must have wondered what was going on. I was slightly taken aback by her question and couldn't respond because I knew deep within me that it was more than just the music.

"You can't feel the presence of God. We live by faith and faith alone!" I have heard so many Believers say those words. Yes, we live by faith. We don't have to feel God because, by faith, we know that He is in us and always with us. but one can experience the tangible presence and power of God. For example, in **Kings 8:11 (ESV)**, "the priests could not stand to minister because of the cloud, for the glory of the Lord filled the house of the Lord." When Paul was on his way to Damascus, he experienced the light of God's glory, fell to the ground, and was blinded **(Acts 9:3-4)**. The face of Moses shone brightly with God's glory when he came down from Mount Sinai after spending 40 days and nights in His presence **(Exodus 34:29)**. On the day of Pentecost, one hundred and twenty people received the promised Holy Spirit and were perceived by others as being drunk **(Acts 2:13)**.

I think it's important to walk with the knowledge and understanding that God still manifests His glory upon people today. I have felt the Holy Spirit come upon me as an electrical sensation, as a gentle breeze zigzagging through my body. Some people feel a warmth come over them. Some are unable to stand in the presence of the Holy Spirit. There are those that weep and laugh. I don't think that our earthly bodies are geared for such power, but one day when we receive our new heavenly bodies, we will experience the fullness of God's glory.

I had felt God's presence in my life many times, had received several healings, but the intensity of His glory upon me that night was beyond anything that I ever experienced. Something happened to me. I received an infilling by the Holy Spirit; I was powered up.

THE TRANSFORMATIVE POWER OF THE HOLY SPIRIT

Several weeks after my encounter, I was at my parent's house watching TV when, out of nowhere, my mother said: "There is something different about you."

Yes, there was! The Holy Spirit had ignited a flame deep within me. I had a joy that was evident to those around me. My countenance was different; there was a peace, a certain glow about me. I had an intense desire to pursue God's calling for my life. I felt an urgency to start speaking about the Holy Spirit, to explain why He was so important in the life of every Believer. Emboldened, I began to share my testimony and talk about Jesus with great ease.

The Holy Spirit equips and prepares all Believers for service; to share with courage and boldness about Jesus.

"But you will receive power when the Holy Spirit comes upon you. And you will be my witnesses, telling people about me everywhere—in Jerusalem, throughout Judea, in Samaria, and to the ends of the earth." (Act 1:8, NLT)

On the day of Pentecost, the Holy Spirit descended upon 120 people. Filled with the Holy Spirit, they began to speak in tongues. Some began mocking them, saying that they were drunk, but Peter, the apostle who had cowered and denied Christ three times, now filled with the Holy Spirit, stepped forward and spoke boldly to the crowd about Jesus and the promise of the Holy Spirit. Three thousand people repented, were baptized in the name of Jesus, and received the gift of the Holy Spirit that day. It was the Holy Spirit at work through Peter.

Believers can experience the infilling power of the Holy Spirit time and time again. For example, in Acts 4:31, the apostles received another infilling by the Holy Spirit, enabling them to speak the Word with boldness and courage. This infilling by the Holy Spirit occurred after the upper room experience!

I have come to understand how important it is to be filled every day with the fresh, anointing power of the Holy Spirit. In those intimate moments with God, the Holy Spirit fills us with abundant love, joy, and peace. He empowers us and helps us face, go through and overcome the many trials and temptations that come our way. We cannot do it on our own strength; we need the help of the Holy Spirit.

"Not by might nor by power, but by my Spirit says the Lord Almighty." (Zechariah 4:6, NIV)

The gift of the Holy Spirit is available to every Believer. In Acts 2: 38-39, Peter replied, **"Repent and be baptized, every one of you, in the name of Jesus Christ for the forgiveness of your sins. And you will receive the gift of the Holy Spirit. The promise is for you and your children and for all who are far off-for all whom the LORD our God will call."**

The Holy Spirit was not only given to the Believers of that specific time, but to all the children of God that would subsequently come to Him, and that includes you and me.

If Jesus needed the Holy Spirit in his ministry, how much more do we need Him now and in the darker days to come. Jesus knew that the Holy Spirit would be crucial in our walk as Believers — He would be our anchor in the storm. That's why He said to his disciples before He returned to the Father:

"But the Helper (Comforter, Advocate, Intercessor, Counselor, Strengthener, Standby), the Holy Spirit, whom the Father will send in My name (in My place, to represent Me and act on My behalf), He will teach you all things. And He will help you remember everything that I have told you." (John 14:16, AMP)

The Holy Spirit on earth is Jesus unlimited. When Jesus was on earth the Holy Spirit walked with Him and was in Him. He was limited to the human body of Jesus. When Jesus left the earth, He gave us an incredible blessed gift—He gave us the Holy Spirit.

We are now Jesus unlimited! How amazing it that! We are His body on earth.

THE ANOINTING
-Saturday, January 10, 2016-

The day after my incredible encounter, the Holy Spirit revealed that God's anointing power was still present on the clothes that I had worn. I was perplexed. Why would He say that to me? As I gently touched the clothes that I had put on my jewelry cabinet the night before, I instantly fell back onto the floor under the power of the Holy Spirit. I remained there for over an hour, immersed once again in indescribable peace. I started to realize that it was not the first time I had experienced the anointing power of the Holy Spirit. He had been slowly teaching me over the years.

In 1992, I was still a consultant for a women's clothing line. Julia, who was married to my cousin Dave, offered to host a party with some ladies from her Church. After the presentation, Julia thought it would be great to have a Bible study and prayer time. We all gathered our chairs and sat close to one another. As Lucinda, the Pastor's wife sat to my right, I heard the soft voice of the Holy Spirit say, "Lay your hand on her back!"

For a moment, I hesitated, but I knew who was speaking to me, and without apprehension, I obeyed. I didn't tell Lucinda what the Holy Spirit had said to me, nor did I ask permission to lay my hand on her. In retrospect, I should have said something because we were both unprepared for what was about to happen. As I gently lay my hand on her upper back, she immediately fell forward to the floor. She turned and looked at me with a puzzled look and said, "Wow! What was that?" She had experienced the tangible power of God—the anointing power of the Holy Spirit.

One afternoon I noticed that our goldfish was floating belly side up in our small aquarium. The Holy Spirit instructed me to put my hands on each side of the aquarium and say: "In the name of Jesus." As I said those words, the fish suddenly flipped over and began to swim. The fish lived for another four months!

In 2010, my friend Sarah and her husband Bob came to the store. They both loved the Lord and had a ministry of their own. There were no customers in the store; it was very quiet. We had a marvelous time talking about Jesus. As I walked with them back to their vehicle, Sarah hugged me and suddenly fell to the ground. I didn't know what was going on. Filled with God's glory, she could hardly walk. Her husband had to hold her as she was laughing and praising God. I didn't understand at that moment what had just happened.

Years later, I accidentally bumped into Sarah in a coffee shop. The first thing that she said to me was,

"Don't hug me; I need to get back to work."

We both started laughing because we remembered what had taken place in the mall.

After reading **Acts 19:6**, I started to understand that the anointing power of the Holy Spirit in a Believer could be imparted unto others. **"When Paul placed his hands on them, the Holy Spirit came on them and they spoke in tongues and prophesied."**

The anointing power of the Holy Spirit is a mystery to me. To see God's glory come upon someone is so wonderful to see. Such an experience transforms, empowers, and strengthens the Believer. You cannot possibly be the same.

-Wednesday, January 14, 2016-

My husband came home from work around 4:30 p.m. and sat in his usual comfy, red-checkered chair. He wasn't feeling well that day; her was experiencing lower abdominal pain.

"Peter, when I had that encounter with God, the clothes that I wore were soaked in His glory. Do you mind if I get my sweater and put it on you?" I said in a serious tone.

"Sure, Carmen," said Peter wincing as he held his belly. I don't think he understood what I was saying, but he always listened to me when I talked about God. He had the faith and belief of a child. So, I quickly went to the bedroom, grabbed the sweater, and gently laid it on his belly. Peter closed his eyes, and instantly I saw a change in his face—there was a glow, a peace that came over him. Then, after a few minutes, I removed the sweater.

"Peter, did you feel anything," I asked as I held on to the sweater with the tip of my fingers. I didn't want to fall over; the anointing was so strong.

"Peace, wow, peace!" Peter whispered. "The pain is all gone."

-Thursday, January 15, 2016-

"Your father is not doing so well. He's having a lot of pain in his lower back. He hasn't moved from his chair since this morning, and that's not like him at all," said my mother worriedly over the phone.

It had been five days since I experienced God's wonderful presence, but I told her all about it and explained that God's anointing power was still on the clothes.

"Come on over, Carmen," replied my mother. She didn't question me at all because she understood that God worked in ways beyond our own human understanding.

"For my thoughts are not your thoughts, nor are your ways my ways, says the Lord. For as the heavens are higher than the earth, so are my ways higher than your ways and my thoughts than your thoughts." (Isaiah 55: 8-9, NLT)

I arrived at my parent's house around 11:30 in the morning, and Dad was still sitting in his comfortable recliner.

"Dad, can you come and sit in this chair," I said as I tried my best to explain about God's anointing power on the clothes and what had happened to me.

"Okay," said Dad, slowly getting up from his recliner to sit on the chair a couple of feet away. He was in so much pain that I think he would have agreed to anything. He wanted to be free of the pain. Mom was standing about five feet from my Dad. As I lay the sweater on his back, I was abruptly pushed back and landed on my derriere a couple of feet away. Mom was startled and asked what had just happened. "Mom, He's here!" I whispered, "God is here! Go towards Dad!"

As she walked in his direction, tears began to flow uncontrollably down her cheeks. She cried softly, "Peace! There's so much peace! I have never felt this before!"

I had never seen my mom exhibiting such emotion; she was experiencing the manifested tangible presence and power of God (the Holy Spirit) for the very first time in her life.

Quietly, I stood up and walked ten feet away, silently praising the Lord. The Holy Spirit taught me a lesson that day. When He is at work, it is never about us! We are simply vessels used for God's glory! The Holy Spirit had merely moved me out of the way.

My father's back felt better within a couple of days, however, he never did say much about that day.

In **Acts 19:12**, we read that God did many miracles through Paul **"so that even handkerchiefs and aprons that had touched him were taken to the sick, and the diseases and evil spirits left."**

In **Acts 5:15**, we read that sick people were brought to the streets in the hope that Peter's shadow might fall upon them as he passed by. Peter had such an intimate relationship with God that the Holy Spirit (the power of God within Him) emanated unto others.

In that three-hour encounter, God's presence upon me was so intense that even the clothes that I wore soaked in His glory. That anointing stayed on the clothes for six days.

It's hard for me to fully comprehend the magnitude of what I experienced that week with the Holy Spirit. Some would even argue that it is impossible, but it did happen, and there were witnesses. Everything that I experienced is biblical. My parents and my husband experienced the anointing power of the Holy Spirit.

God has given us such a wonderful gift, the Holy Spirit. I now understand the depth of what that means. We are carriers of God's glory. The same power that raised Jesus from the grave lives in every Believer. Jesus said to his disciples:

"I tell you the truth, anyone who believes in me will do the same works that I have done and even greater works because I am going to be with the Father. You can ask for anything in my name, and I will do it so that the Son can bring glory to the Father." (John 14:12-13, NLT)

The following is a prayer that was written by Walter Julius Carey, who was the Bishop of Bloemfontein in South Africa from 1921 to 1934. A prayer for those who hunger for a fresh infilling of the Holy Spirit:

"Holy Spirit of God, come again to my heart and fill me. I open the windows of my soul to let thee in, come and possess me, fill me with light and truth. Of myself, I am an unprofitable servant, an empty vessel. Fill me that I may live the life of thy Spirit, the life of truth and goodness, the life of wisdom and strength, the life of beauty and love. And guide me today in all things, guide me to the people I should meet and help, to the circumstances in which I may best serve, whether by my actions or by my suffering. But above all, make Christ to be formed in me, that I may dethrone self in my heart and make Him King. Bind me to Christ by all ways, known and unknown, by holy thoughts, and unseen graces, and sacramental ties, that He may be in me, and I in Him, this day and forever."

CHAPTER 30

CLOSING THE BOUTIQUE

-March 2016-

After ten years, Peter and I decided to close "On the Go Fashions." The timing was perfect because I knew God had other plans for me, but I was worried; I didn't want to leave in debt and be stuck with a lot of inventory.

"I'll close my store, and do as you asked of me, but my only request is not to leave in debt," I pleaded to the Lord.

On the first day of our closing out sale, I had three of my friends helping in the store. To my surprise, a considerable crowd had gathered outside. For security reasons, we could only let ten people in at a time. It was busy, and there was a lot of excitement in the air as people hurriedly grabbed merchandise and proceeded to the check-out line with mounds of clothing and jewelry in their arms. By the end of the week, I had one rack of clothing and a few boxes of miscellaneous items left.

One afternoon, I was busy cleaning the store when I heard a knock at the door. It was my friend Lil.

"Carmen, I need your help. My daughter is getting married next week, and I can't find anything," said Lil as she entered the store. "I need a dress, a pair of shoes, and a necklace."

"I don't have too much left, Lil, just one rack of clothes, some jewelry with a few pairs of shoes at the back," I sadly replied.

"Well, show me what you have," said Lil in her usual bubbly way. I wanted to help, but I hardly had anything left.

Miraculously, I managed to find everything she was looking for and, of course, gave her a good deal! Lil was blown away and so grateful that she had come to the store.

I was so thankful to God that I could bless one more person in those last few hours before permanently closing the store. The liquidation sale had been an enormous success, and because of that, I was able to leave the store three weeks earlier than expected. And praise the Lord, I was also debt-free!

Adapting to change can be difficult, and it sure was for me. In that first year following the store's closure, I attempted three times to re-open, but every time I went to sign a new lease, I started feeling anxious and irritable. I couldn't sign on that dotted line. I quickly realized that every time I was out of God's will, I was miserable.

God had a plan for my life, but He would have to break me from my continuous need for self-validation, which came from my ability to sell things and make money. I enjoyed being busy; I missed being around people, serving them, and making them feel good. I was having such a hard time getting used to not having a store!

"Carmen, I don't want you to open another store. You had a great time with On the Go. You climbed your mountain, you did well, but it's time to move on," said my husband as I tried to persuade him otherwise.

Okay, I was upset, but I knew he was right, and deep down, I was glad to hear him say that. Peter always supported me in everything that I did, but this time he put his foot down, and that's what I needed. Finally, one day, out of frustration, I cried out to God and said: "Lord, can you please take away this desire that I have to sell things and make money all the time."

Shortly after that prayer, I decided to dive back into the home party scene. I bought kits to sell jewelry, purses, and clothes, but I didn't have any ambition to do anything with them when they arrived. So, I sent them all back! My desire to sell things, make money or even open another store was completely gone. I couldn't even sell a pen! God had removed all those desires from me!

There are times when God will move us in another direction, and when that happens, we need to trust Him fully. That can be a difficult thing to do, but through obedience, He can precipitate great changes that will impact not only you but others as well!

CHAPTER 31

HUNGERING FOR THE PRESENCE OF GOD

I hungered for more of God and dove into the Word, wanting to know more about this wonderful third person of the trinity, the Holy Spirit. I was like a sponge, absorbing everything about Him. I read books and watched videos of other ministries that knew of Him such as Kathryn Kuhlman, Dr. Charles Stanley, Benny Hinn, and many more. The Holy Spirit would reveal much to me about the anointing, the PRESENCE of God, the POWER of God and the PERSON of Jesus. He was my greatest teacher.

BEING STILL

"Be still and know (recognize, understand) that I am God." (Psalm 46:10, AMP)

One day, Jesus and His disciples went to a village called Bethany, where a woman named Martha welcomed them into her home. Martha was busy and distracted with hosting duties, while her sister Mary sat at the feet of Jesus, listening, and absorbing everything He was saying. Martha complained to Jesus that she was doing all the work and asked Him to tell her sister to help.

"Martha, Martha," the Lord answered, "you are worried and upset about many things, but few things are needed—or indeed only one. Mary has chosen what is better, and it will not be taken away from her." (Luke 10: 41-42, NIV)

Mary got it! She knew that the only thing that mattered was to be with Jesus. His presence satisfied her very soul.

Being still has not always been easy for me because of cyclothymia. The greatest challenge in my prayer life was slowing down my wandering mind. So, I needed to find a place of quietness away from everything and everyone. That special place was usually the bathroom or downstairs in my music studio.

Because I am so easily distracted, I need to make sure that my cellphone is not within my reach and that the ringer is off. I usually use an iPad for music, sing at the piano or prefer being in total silence.

I have often felt God's tangible presence while praising and worshipping Him. Usually, when that happens, I sense a shift taking place in the atmosphere. There is a lightness in the air and an indescribable peace within and around me.

Often, I have stopped playing and have fallen to my knees, trembling, and weeping in His presence. For in that place of holiness, one acknowledges the blood of Jesus, the sacrifice paid upon the cross for the atonement of one's sins. There is a cleansing, a purification taking place within one's soul, followed by a holy silence, where you cannot utter a word. In that silence, God starts ministering to your soul. You feel His presence upon your very being, overflowing into you. Time goes by, and all you care about is being in His presence. Enwrapped in His perfect love, His perfect peace, you experience a joy bursting from within.

As you draw near to God, He draws nearer to you and reveals Himself to you in many ways. God knows everything about you **(James 4:8)**. He knows what you are going to say even before you open your mouth. He sees the very core of your heart **(Psalm 139:1-4)**. He is interested in every aspect of your life: your friends, your relationships, your finances, your children, your family, your hopes and dreams, and more! God seeks to have a relationship with you, and He will pursue you, make His presence known to you in such wonderful ways!

WORLD OF DISTRACTIONS

The world has changed so much over the years. The greatest threat to the human soul has been in the advancement of digital technologies. Why? Because it keeps people busy and distracted all the time. Satan, a.k.a. the enemy of man's soul, desires to keep people so captivated and engrossed by these technologies that they are blinded from the truth, unable to be still and ponder about God, about their very soul and where they will be for eternity. I am not saying that it's wrong to have a computer or cell phone, but we need time in God's presence. I am guilty at times of being too much on my gadgets, but nothing is more important, believe me when I say that. The time is drawing near. Jesus is coming back, but His Bride is not ready! What will you do when you stand before Him? What excuse will you have? I love Him, yet I fear Him. He is a God who loves us dearly, but Jesus is coming, and there will be judgment. Are we ready?

In 2019, the Holy Spirit lay upon my heart that many Believers have great difficulty in finding time to be with God. They have a desire to have a closer relationship with Him yet struggle with inner hurts and demands from the world around them. God wants our time, wants us to come to Him in trueness of heart. He wants us to trust Him with every single detail of our lives. This is the song I was inspired to write:

"THE RHYTM OF YOUR HEART"

I can't hear Your voice through the storms in my life
I know You're here, but I'm drowning inside
Pull me in You're my hiding place

I want to be closer to You
I want to feel, the rhythm,
the rhythm of Your Heart

Fill me with Your Love to never be the same
To never be the same
Fill me with Your peace to never be the same
To never be the same

I want to let You in through all these walls of hurts
Pierce me with Your love, heal this broken vessel
To give my all, my all to You… Lord

I want to be closer to You
I want to feel, the rhythm,
the rhythm of Your Heart

Fill me with Your Love to never be the same
To never be the same
Fill me with Your peace to never be the same
To never be the same

I want to be closer to You
I want to feel, the rhythm,
the rhythm of Your Heart

Copyright 2019, CC Harvey Music.

CHAPTER 32

BACK TO THE MUSIC

After the boutique's closure, I strongly desired to write and compose music again. Sixteen years had passed since the release of my last album, and now I began working on a new album and single called: "Let it Rain." I recorded that song in three different languages (French, English, and Spanish). This song meant a lot to me since it was about Believers calling upon the Holy Spirit to empower and heal them.

"LET IT RAIN"

Holy Spirit, I need you today
Holy Spirit flow through me now
Heal my broken heart, before I fall apart
For, I am human, and I can't take it anymore
I need you now

So many times, I've called Your name
Here I am Lord down on my knees
Let it rain…
Rain… rain…rain
Let Your Spirit rain on me

Holy Spirit, I need you today
Holy Spirit flow through me now
Heal my body's pain, please break these chains
For, I am human, and I can't take it anymore
I need you now

So many times, I've called your name
Here I am Lord down on my knees
Let it rain…
Rain… rain…rain
Let Your Spirit rain on me

Holy…… Holy…... Holy
Let Your Spirit rain on me

Holy Spirit, I need You today
Holy Spirit flow through me now…

Copyright 2016, CC Harvey Music.

It was unbelievable how everything came together. I was able to find Jeff Nelson, an incredible Christian Producer, and Arranger from Jeff Nelson Productions in Nashville, Tennessee. Jeff had collaborated with many known Christian Artists throughout his career and was a gifted pianist. Since he knew a lot of top industry musicians, I was blessed to have many of them play in my songs. I just dove into the music, writing, composing, and recording songs for the album. I practiced and played the piano daily, worshipping and praising the Lord, and spent much time in the Word.

DISILLUSIONED

I experienced many trials along the way, but God continued to refine and define me as He prepared me for service. I would be profoundly wounded by many who call themselves Christians, those who profess to love the Lord, but in those times of closeness with God, the Holy Spirit would comfort me, give me the strength to endure, persevere, and overcome. I don't know what I would have done without the Holy Spirit. Had I known the trials ahead of me, I think I would have run the other way. But, of course, I never did. The trials are worth it; believe me when I say that. I have not regretted my decision to accept His calling upon my life. I long to be in His presence and enjoy seeing the outpouring of His glory upon people.

During that time, I was so happy to find a church where I could worship and have fellowship with other Believers. Unfortunately, it was not what I anticipated. I found it extremely difficult to fit in, to break through the little cliques within the Church. I had been attending with one of my aunts for over six months, yet hardly anyone spoke to us or invited us to any church activities. No one made any attempts to make us feel accepted, and we were both social butterflies!

One evening, my daughter accompanied me to a women's bible study held on the second floor. All the ladies were sitting around a table as we entered the room. No one greeted us as we sat down, and no one spoke to us afterward. I am sure that if I had engaged in conversation with someone, they would have responded, but it's hard to talk when ignored. As newbies to the group, I thought they would have been more welcoming toward us, but this would repeatedly happen. After the bible study, KD and I went down to the main foyer to get our coats. I was heartbroken and so disappointed.

"What is wrong with these people! I am a Child of God, yet I don't even feel like I belong here," I angrily said as I looked up. I didn't realize that someone from the group was looking at us. She had overheard everything yet quietly turned and walked away. I felt hurt—I felt alone!

The Church that I remember from my youth was full of God's love. Something was missing—the Holy Spirit! To reach out to others in love, we need the Holy Spirit. A Church will grow when love is present. People will feel accepted when love is present.

"I am giving you a new commandment, that you love one another. Just as I have loved you, so you too are to love one another. By this everyone will know that you are My disciples if you have love and unselfish concern for one another." (John 13:34-35, AMP)

A dead church becomes alive when the Holy Spirit is present because the fruit of the Spirit manifests itself through its members.

It was a terrible time for me because I kept discerning an absence of God's Spirit within the Church, and therefore was deeply troubled and disillusioned!

CHAPTER 33

WOUNDED BY WORDS

WE ARE ALL VALUABLE MEMBERS OF GOD'S KINGDOM

I had an intense desire, a burning within me to serve God. I attended Church for quite some time and decided to ask one of the leaders if I could help in some capacity.

"Yes, that would be great, we will call you," said the Pastor, but nothing ever came of it. Meanwhile, I continued writing and composing songs at home and spent many hours worshipping the Lord at the piano.

One evening, while at bible study, I was sitting quietly in the pew when the Holy Spirit told me that a man in our group had a heart condition. With that revelation, I decided to go and pray for him. I should have waited for the prompting by the Holy Spirit because I was unprepared for what was to unfold. His wife was sitting in a pew at the front of the sanctuary when I approached her. "Can I pray for your husband?" I said with confidence. "The Holy Spirit told me that your husband has a heart condition."

"Oh, is that right, sure! Let me ask the Pastor," she replied.

When everyone had agreed that it was okay for me to pray, a group of six people gathered. They had no prior knowledge of anything being wrong with his heart. As I began to pray for him, I felt God's glory come upon me. It was as though the heavens had opened; an invisible beam encircled me. Immersed within it, I felt a lightness in the air. The intensity was far greater than what I had experienced in my three-hour encounter with God. I was about three feet away from her husband when I began to pray aloud. I did not lay hands on him, but while praying, his wife put her hand on my back and began screeching. I sensed that something was not right. I immediately had a vision in which I saw a white background with red lettering that said: "SPIRIT CHECK."

What am I supposed to do now? I thought to myself. As a Believer, I knew that we battled against unknown principalities, but I was unprepared. I was way over my head, and God knew!

I kept thinking to myself, *how do I get out of this?*

I was between the husband and the wife when I suddenly found myself twenty feet away from where I was. I turned around and saw the wife praying over the husband. That's all I remember. I was there—then I wasn't. She could barely stand; it was as though she was "drunk." Two people had to carry her out of the sanctuary.

The Holy Spirit explained that darkness could not abide in the presence of God's glory. As she lay her hand on me, the power of God (the Holy Spirit) came upon her, and the evil spirit within her cried out and fled from the light.

A friend of mine asked me later how I ended up twenty feet away. I casually replied, "God removed me." God was there. He heard my distress and came to my rescue! The Spirit of God had miraculously transported me twenty feet away! In **Acts 8:26-40**, Philip led an Ethiopian eunuch to faith in Christ. After the eunuch was baptized, **"the Spirit of the Lord suddenly took Philip away and the eunuch did not see him again but went on his way rejoicing. Philip, however appeared at Azotus" (verses 39-40).** That was for sure an instance of miraculous transportation.

I have come to understand that with God nothing is impossible.

As they carried the wife out of the sanctuary, one of the leaders came to me and said:

"Carmen, you didn't do anything wrong. I'm going to speak to her about this."

I was troubled by those words because I knew I hadn't done anything wrong; I had prayed over someone.

"Please don't, I gently replied. "The Holy Spirit will take care of it. When the Holy Spirit is at work, everything that He does is in absolute perfection."

Unfortunately, he didn't listen to my advice and there would be repercussions.

I believe that God allowed me to have this experience to teach me about spiritual warfare. I was also taught a great lesson—not to move ahead of the Holy Spirit. I was unprepared for what took place. Because of that experience, I began to understand that Believers could be under the influence of demonic powers. So, I dove into the Word to determine if that could be possible. In **Matthew 10:1-8**, Jesus called his twelve disciples together and gave them authority to cast out evil spirits and heal people. He did not send them to the Gentiles or Samaritans; He sent them to the people of Israel, God's lost sheep. Then, in **Mark 1:39**, Jesus went from one synagogue to the next to preach and cast out demons. He was delivering religious people, those who loved God and lived according to the law of Moses. These people lived at a higher standard of holiness, and Jesus was delivering them. In **Matthew 16**, Jesus said to Peter, "Satan get behind me." Satan had influenced Peter, a Believer. In **John 13:27**, "when Judas had eaten the bread, Satan entered into Him." Judas was also a Believer. In **Acts 5:1-3**, we have a spirit-filled Believer, Ananias who, with his wife, Sapphira lied to the Holy Spirit when they sold some property and brought part of the money to the apostle. So, Peter said, "Ananias, why have you let Satan fill your heart?" Therefore, according to Scripture, I have concluded that a Spirit-filled Believer can be under the power of demonic influences.

When you are a Believer in Christ, no demonic spirit can touch your human spirit because that is where the Spirit of God (the Holy Spirit) resides—it is a holy place. However, demons can affect a Believer in the soul realm, which consists of our thoughts, our mind, will and emotions.

I cried and pleaded to God that evening for the husband, for I knew that his wife had received the blessing. The Holy Spirit had told me so.

Believers should only lay hands on someone when led by the Holy Spirit, not out of pride or selfish motive.

On the Sunday of that week, my husband and I went to Church. We were greeted at the door by the man I had prayed for during the week and his wife. He was very kind and thanked me for praying over him.

I playfully said, "Yeah, your wife got the blessing!" Those words did not resonate well with her. She became angry and vehemently said, "What do you mean? I was the intercessor!"

She followed us to the vestibule, and as we took off our coats, she looked intently at me and said in a threatening way, "This is not over! We will speak about this later!" Slightly shaken by her unkind words, I began to tremble inside. I never had in my life encountered this sort of behavior. My poor husband was dumbfounded!

"I will speak to you if led by the Holy Spirit," I boldly said as we walked towards the sanctuary. I was full of anxiety. So much so that it was difficult for me to pay attention and listen to the sermon. Midway through the service, the Holy Spirit said to me: "Leave!" I didn't listen because I was worried about what others would say. But, in retrospect, I should have obeyed because the Holy Spirit was trying to protect me.

After the service, the man in a leadership position, the same man who witnessed the occurrence on Wednesday night, stood at the doorway, greeting people as they left the sanctuary. He took both my elbows with his hands and drew me towards him as I approached. He whispered in my left ear: "What you are doing at home; you are doing too much of." *What does he mean? I thought to myself. All I do at home is praise and worship the Lord and study the Word.* He said something else to me, but I have lost all recollection of those words.

Was he afraid of the anointing power of the Holy Spirit? Did someone approach him? Did he speak to the wife? I thought to myself at the time. Those spoken words pierced my soul; hurt me so much that

I had difficulty praising and worshiping God at the piano. It felt like I was in a mud puddle, unable to move forward.

Stricken with impenetrable grief, it took several weeks for me to recover from those words. While sitting on the sofa in the living room one morning, the Holy Spirit instructed me to write a letter. So, I did! As I began to write and pour my heart unto paper, the oppression upon me lifted. I then realized that the enemy (Satan) had used that man in position of leadership to spiritually derail me.

I am slowly learning to discern when the enemy is at work. Satan hates Believers and will try his best to stop God's plan and purpose for their lives, especially those in ministry. That is why it is so important to put on the full armor of God **(Ephesians 6:14-17)**.

It took me two months to return to Church, but I was on my guard from further hurts. The woman who had offended my husband and I approached me one Sunday morning as the congregants were greeting one another.

"Carmen, can you please forgive me? You were right. My husband had a heart condition. We went for a walk in the park one day, and he collapsed. His heart stopped five times that day, and they were able to bring him back," said the woman as she embraced me. I could tell that she felt terrible about the whole situation.

"Yes, I forgive you, of course! Praise the Lord," I joyously replied. Our hearts reconciled; no other words had to be said. I was thankful that God had his hand of protection over her husband.

It was a difficult time for me. I would continue to be shunned and offended by those in leadership positions. I often wondered if it was because I was a woman in ministry. Regardless, I decided to move forward with the calling that God had put upon my heart. In faith, I designed a ministry website called: "CC Harvey Ministries." Our mission was to empower Believers to walk victoriously in the anointing power of the Holy Spirit. I would forge ahead no matter the obstacles that lay before me. Though misunderstood by many in Church, the Holy Spirit would lead me to share the gospel of Jesus Christ, to pray and uplift Believers. Time and time again, I would see God's mighty hand at work. I would see the moving of the Holy Spirit not within the box of a building that we call Church, but outside of its very walls. I would see Believers experience the tangible presence of God as they prayed and worshiped Him.

I learned that the wounds inflicted by others do not define me. I know who I am in Christ. I know who God says I am. It says in the Word of God that we are all God's royal priests. We are redeemed, chosen, and adopted by a loving Father.

"But you are a chosen people, a royal priesthood, a holy nation, God's special possession, that you may declare the praises of him who called you out of darkness into his wonderful light." (1 Peter 2:9, NIV)

We are God's messengers to the world. As priests, we help others in the Kingdom fulfill their calling (purpose, destiny) in Christ. We teach and uplift one another in the love of Christ, putting away all strife and jealousy amongst us as we bear the fruit of the Spirit of God. We are all valuable members of His Kingdom.

"But the fruit of the Spirit is love, joy, peace, long-suffering, kindness, goodness, faithfulness, gentleness, self-control." (Galatians 5:22-23, NIV)

We all labor together in unity— in one Spirit!

I believe from the depth of my being that when the Glory of God begins to fall like never before upon the Church, we will see many come to salvation, demons cast out, people healed, prophetic words spoken, speaking in tongues and interpretation of tongues. People will experience the transformative power and love of God. You will see Believers set afire for Jesus, and they will be a light shining bright in this ever-so-darkening world. Unbelievers will see Jesus, and God will be glorified.

The Holy Spirit inspired me to write this song in 2020, about a loving God who pursues us, loves our individualities, and understands our pain.

"I AM HUMAN"

Sometimes I feel so sad
Sometimes I'm so mad
It's not right to feel this way, they say
I am human, not a robot
Flesh and blood, full of emotions
Intricately woven by the Master's hands,
and He knows who I am

Don't need religious indoctrinations,
legalistic manipulations
Just want to be free to worship thee, Lord
I am human, not a robot
Flesh and blood, full of emotions
Intricately woven by the Master's hands,
and on His Word, I'll stand

In my despair, you are there
You pursue me,
because You love me, as I am

I feel I'm in a cage, staring at a stage
There's so much more in Jesus so much more
When His Spirit stirs, I will answer the call
Won't let the fear of men keep me in that cell
I am human, not a robot
Flesh and blood, full of emotions
Intricately woven by the Master's hands,
and He knows who I am

Copyright 2020, CC Harvey Music.

CHAPTER 34

ANGELIC INTERVENTION

-August 2016-

My daughter KD and I had planned a four-day vacation to Quebec City. I was looking forward to this special time together.

On our first day, we spontaneously decided to go on a five-hour bus tour of Quebec City. Our first stop was at Parc de la Chute-Montmorency Falls, a spectacular historical site boasting an 83-meter-high waterfall almost 100 feet higher than Niagara Falls.

As the bus came to a halt, we decided that we would ride the gondola to view the majestic falls.

The conductor stood beside the bus giving each passenger a free ticket for the aerial tram. As I stepped off the bus, I was unaware that one of the sidewalk slabs two feet ahead of me was uneven. I lost my balance when my right foot caught the elevation, which caused my whole body to propel itself forward. My daughter stood there with a puzzled look on her face. She thought that I was racing ahead to get on the gondola.

Oh my goodness, I'm in trouble; one hundred and ninety-five pounds of me will hit that pavement, and I'm going to be hurt, I thought to myself.

As soon as that thought entered my mind, I felt a nudge on the left side of my hip, but there wasn't anyone there. That little push caused a change in the direction of my fall. Instead of falling forward, my whole body turned forty-five degrees to face the bus. The right side of my forehead hit the bus as both my legs went down in a kneeling position.

I suffered significant surface abrasions below both knees, as well as the knuckles of both hands. There was a lot of blood, but thankfully there were no broken bones! I was in a state of shock and momentarily confused by the incident.

"Mom, do you want us to call an ambulance?" said KD with a concerned look on her face.

"No, I'll be fine!" I quickly interjected, but I was not really in a good state. I just didn't want to ruin our trip, and KD knew that convincing me to go to the hospital would be a losing battle.

A young man standing beside his bicycle had seen the fall and quickly came to help. He gave us two six-inch bandages. They were the exact size needed to cover the wounds on my knees. That was no coincidence!

I was slightly disoriented and could feel my body trembling inside as KD helped me to the washroom.

"Mom are you sure you're okay?" said KD as she gently cleansed my wounds and applied the bandages.

"I'm okay," I said as my eyes welled up with tears. "Let's go up the gondola before we run out of time.

I looked rough with my torn bloody jean, scraped-up knuckles, and bandaged knees. I was still shaking inside, my legs felt like jelly, and I was in excruciating pain as we went up the gondola, but KD held on to me.

God gave me the mental and physical strength to endure the rest of our vacation. I was fortunate that my daughter was a Nurse; it made me feel more at ease. Although it was difficult for me to walk, I still managed to do many activities such as the *Ghost Walk* and go down the three-hundred and ninety-three steps of the *Cap-Blanc Stairs of Old Quebec City*.

I had a fantastic time with my daughter, thanks to a wonderful, loving God who sent an angel to change the direction of my fall.

"For he will command his angels concerning you to guard you in all your ways." (Psalm 91:11, NIV)

My daughter witnessed this mind-boggling miracle. She told me that she was amazed by the orchestration of the fall and the strength seen in her mother, a strength that only God could have given.

CHAPTER 35

SHOOK TO THE CORE

Post-Rapture Dream
-First Dream, November 15th, 2016-

I was in a dream, sitting near the edge of a long pew in church. There were a few gauntly looking people scattered about; some had their heads down, silently praying, while others stared ahead as though in a daze. Something was not quite right. The silence was unbearable. To my left was a young woman lying in a fetal position. She was petrified of someone or something.

"Everything is going to be alright," I calmly reassured her, but she couldn't see or hear me—I was only there in spirit.

Two men dressed in black suits entered the room from a door located at the front left side of the sanctuary. I knew that they were coming for these people — I knew that their lives were in danger. Suddenly, I was no longer there but taken to another dream.

-Second Dream, November 15th, 2016-

I saw many people standing in a single file row in front of a small-- framed man squatting on a platform. One by one, they approached to kiss his outstretched right hand. I couldn't see his face since he was looking down.

"No. I will never pledge allegiance to you," I yelled from a short distance away.

Nobody heard me, for I was there only in spirit. I instantly found myself standing to the left of the man on the platform. As I looked down, I saw what appeared to be two bony stubs on his upper back, covered with a velvety brown hue. The left side of his light brown face revealed his whitish-gray sideburn and a short afro hairstyle. I noticed his ear; it was longer and narrower than a normal ear. Most unexpectedly, I found myself standing before him, and as he slowly lifted his head, I saw his face. It's not important for me to describe it, but to say that he had mesmerizing, clear, light blue eyes that gave the impression of gentleness and kindness, but I knew he was a wolf in sheep's clothing. He was not to be trusted; he would deceive many.

DREAM OF HELL
-Third Dream, November 16th, 2016-

I awoke early in the morning shaken by a dreadful dream. In this dream, I was in a house surrounded by elegantly dressed people; men in tuxedos and women wearing expensive evening gowns. They were busy talking amongst themselves, laughing, and having a fun time. They all had a glass of wine or a martini in their hand.

From afar, I saw a demon come out of a wall. I only saw it from the waist up; its lower limbs were still within the wall. As this creature grabbed one of the men in the room, the wall immediately closed behind them. I didn't see what he was doing, but somehow, I knew that the demon was tearing him apart, that he was going through indescribable torment.

Everyone was oblivious to what was happening as they partied away, but these demons would torment all, one by one, for eternity. I believe that what I saw in hell was a place of torment for those who lived a life of self-indulgence.

I looked out of a window and saw huge, dangling, linked chains cascading down from wherever this place was in hell. Each chain had hundreds of people bound to it. Like zombies, the people looked lifeless, dangling there amidst billows of smoke rising from below. It was a place of death, of doom.

I suddenly found myself standing beside a wall. The wall opened like a black portal, revealing a demonic figure. It could not see me, for I was there in spirit. I only saw it from the chest up. He didn't have any clothes on his body.

He had reptilian-like features, hairless dark brownish-green skin, long narrow arms with fingers that had eight-inch blade-like nails like Wolverine in X-Men. He had deep, cold, lifeless black eyes and sharp, two-inch-long, jagged teeth.

I awoke from this dream, shaken and trembling under my blankets. "Please, God," I cried out. "Don't ever let me go there again." This dream was so horrible that I didn't speak to anyone about it for three months.

Several months following this dream, I visited a friend who spoke to me about a supernatural being that she had seen roaming in her hallway one night. I drew a picture of the demon I saw in the wall. She took the paper in her hands, then looked at me with big eyes and said, "Oh my goodness, I have goosebumps all over. That is exactly what I saw in my hallway." She couldn't believe it.

The Bible warns us of a place called hell. There are many references in the New Testament with warnings of hell, and many of these references were uttered by Jesus.

"Do not be afraid of those who kill the body but cannot kill the soul. Rather, be afraid of the One who can destroy both soul and body in hell." (Matthew 10:28, NIV)

CHAPTER 36

END TIME SONG

Although shaken by those dreams, they were given to me for a reason. God's timing is always perfect. During that time, I was working on the "Let It Rain" album, and I needed one more song to complete it.

In December 2017, a month following those unsettling dreams, the Holy Spirit told me to go into my music binder to retrieve one of the two end-time songs that I had written in 1996. As I sat at the piano, a new chorus and melody were given to me by the Holy Spirit. I sang the song several times, paused, then asked the Holy Spirit,

"Who is this song for?"

"For those who will be left behind," he replied.

I fell to my knees and wept. I believe that God gave me those dreams to give me a burden for souls. God loves us so much. He doesn't want anyone to perish, however He has given us free will, but on that day, when we stand before Him, there will be no excuse.

"What Will You Do If You Are Left Behind," written under the guidance of the Holy Spirit, is a song with a powerful message of hope and salvation in Jesus Christ for those left behind during the Great Tribulation. This song is to stir people's hearts, to make them reflect upon their walk, where they stand in their relationship with God.

"WHAT WILL YOU DO IF YOU ARE LEFT BEHIND"

What will you do in the days of persecution?
Will you turn around and flee?
Will you deny Him as your King?
Will the rooster crow

Will you fall from His grace?
Will you fall from His grace?
Or hold on tight to God's loving arms
Remember the cross
Keep reading His word
Though the Spirit of God be gone
Standfast unto Him
Jesus will hear your cry
He will hear your cry

What will you do if you are left behind?
Will you stand by His word?
Will you take the mark of the beast?
For a loaf of bread

Will you fall from His grace?
Will you fall from His grace?
Or hold on tight to God's loving arms
Remember the cross
Keep reading His word
Though the Spirit of God be gone
Standfast unto Him
Jesus will hear your cry
He will hear your cry
Don't fall from His grace

ALWAYS NEVER ALONE

Don't fall from His grace
Hold on tight to God's loving arms

Remember the cross
Keep reading His word
Though the Spirit of God be gone Standfast
Standfast unto Him
Jesus will hear your cry
He will hear your cry
What will you do if you are left behind…?

Copyright 1996, 2017, CC Harvey Music.

CHAPTER 37

END TIME MUSIC VIDEO

God put upon my heart in November of 2017 to produce a video for the song: "What Will You Do If You Are Left Behind," four months after the "Let it Rain" album's release in July 2017. I felt that the Holy Spirit wanted a specific married couple for this video; however, it would take two years for them to be available and for everything to fall into place. Through that waiting, I realized that the timing for this video was in God's hands, not mine.

We officially started filming in August 2019. As we individually approached people, they all enthusiastically agreed to volunteer their time. We had ten people altogether. Some of the volunteers didn't have any acting experience yet conveyed tremendous emotions in many of the scenes.

In August 2019, my friend Linda from Southern Ontario was the first to be filmed.

Instructed to sit behind the steering wheel, Linda conveyed the desperation, the grief, the fear of being "left behind." As I began filming, Linda started crying and hitting the steering wheel. She expressed such deep emotion that tears began to roll down my cheeks. I wanted to stop filming, but the Holy Spirit softly whispered: "Don't stop filming; she's getting into character." It was heart-wrenching for me to film because it felt so real. I am happy that I listened to the Holy Spirit because it was one of the most emotional scenes captured.

The hell scene required in the video was a bit more challenging. The flames were filmed from the fire pit at our cottage and zoomed in before superimposing the hands. Rebecca, my daughter's friend, and Sylvie, a long time friend volunteered for this scene. Lying on the ground, on their backs, I instructed them to lift their arms up and put their fingers in a claw-like position to depict agony. Sylvie had some difficulties with this scene. She kept waving her hands back and and forth as though in worship. I had to say to her:"Sylvie, you are in hell being tormented; stop with the praise hands!" We all started laughing. As I lay there beside them, I filmed the scene from their elbows up.

We shed many tears and had great laughs throughout this project, and a few people realized that they had hidden talents. For example, my cousin Gerianne who volunteered to shoot several scenes had minimal videography skills yet captured unforgettable moments.

We were family, unified in Christ, working together for Kingdom purpose.

The official release of the video was January 18th, 2020. Thanks to donations by several people, our ministry was able to promote this video on various social media platforms. Since its release, over fifteen thousand people have seen the video, and our goal is to continue promoting this video to reach millions.

From the moment we started this project, we could feel God's peace and presence. The most memorable scene was captured at Halfmoon Lake in Timmins, Ontario. In that particular scene, Bill one of the main actors is reading the Bible to three ladies sitting on a log in front of him. Since it was a very cold day,

Bill had to start a fire as the ladies covered themselves with a warm blanket. Gerianne was filming at one end and I at the other. Suddenly, as we were filming, a beam of light pierced through the trees and landed right into the fire pit. We were able to capture it at the right moment.

Undoubtedly, this is a sign from God that He is pleased with us, I thought to myself.

We are not always privy to God's plans and purposes, but I have learned that He will never call us to do something we can't do. I don't know who will be blessed by this video, but as I stand before God one day, all will be made known. What a glorious day that will be!

www.ccharveyministries.com/end-time-ministry

CHAPTER 38

WHEN YOU ARE CALLED

When you receive a revelation of your calling from God, it can take years for the Holy Spirit to get you ready. He will use your talents, your abilities and teach you along the way. God will equip you. When you move in the direction of your calling, your desire to serve Him will become stronger. You will be at peace. When you move in a direction against your calling, you will feel a struggle within. You will feel unhappy and distant from Him. When God calls you for service, you can't ignore it. You know that He has called you because there is a burning desire within you to pursue what He has put on your heart. There will be moments when you will have doubts, apprehensions, but the Holy Spirit will counsel, and guide you along the way.

The enemy will try to attack you with your mind, but keep yourself grounded in the Word, and God will direct your path. The Holy Spirit will be your greatest teacher.

> "I will instruct you and teach you in the way you should go; I will counsel you with my loving eye on you."
> **Psalm 32:8 New (NIV)**

If God has a calling on your life, my advice is to jump right in with both feet and fully trust Him. He will open doors and bring the right people into your life.

"Trust in the Lord with all your heart and lean not on your own understanding; in all your ways submit to him, and he will make your paths straight." Proverbs 3:5-6 (NIV)

CHAPTER 39

FINALLY LETTING GO OF THE PAIN

In the summer of 2021, I invited my sister Claire to spend the day at our cottage. There were a lot of annoying black flies, typical for that time of the year, so we hurried inside. We sat facing each other on the long sofa, and as we sipped our hot teas, we rambled on about life, our past, and the wonderful memories of our childhood. We talked about the future and the blessing of having grandchildren. After a while, I began to share what happened to me as a child. It was not the first time I had confided in her about the assault, I had done so many times before, but it was different this time. Tears welled up in my eyes as I recounted that day. I started sobbing profoundly as my sister held me in her arms.

"The bastard!" I cried out. "I shouldn't say that I'm so sorry." "You have every right to say that. It's okay," said Claire, full of compassion. She knew that I needed to say those words out loud.

My sister was there to listen, comfort and understand my pain, and in so doing, I was able to let go and finally free myself of the pain. God had used my sister that day to enable me to let go because He knew that it was the time for me to do so.

Years prior, in my late twenties, I had confided in someone, but because that individual showed no compassion, my defense walls went up, and the pain buried itself deeper within my heart.

Fellowship is so important amongst the Believers. It says in **Galatians 6:2** to bear one another's burdens, and that is so important. When you pour out your heart to someone who is receptive, there is a release for healing to occur.

Compassion is love poured on an open wound, helping it heal from the inside out.

EPILOGUE

I've had many trials in my life, and God had to heal many broken parts of me. He revealed Himself to me in ways that are difficult for me to comprehend and explain fully, but I have tried to the best of my abilities. I cannot deny all I have experienced with the Holy Spirit because it has forever changed me! Through the soft whispers of the Holy Spirit, I have come to know God's voice, and through that friendship, God's love for me was made known. I have been a witness to the power of the Holy Spirit. I have felt God's presence and glory upon me. There is absolutely nothing in this world that can ever fulfill me. I hunger for His presence, for His infilling power in my life. There will always be storms that I will have to face and go through, but the Holy Spirit will always be there to guide, comfort and teach me. There will always be these battles in my mind, but this I know. I am and will always be a child of God, a daughter of a King who loves me, who has my back.

I am nobody special to this world, but my Heavenly Father graciously reached out to me many years ago through a dream and told me that I would *never be alone*, that *He would always be with me*. I did not understand the depth of that dream until years later. God spoke to me that night because he saw my brokenness and reached out to me. Throughout my life, God was there to give me the strength and the courage to go on, especially in those seasons of my life when I had none. I know that I am loved by Him, and truly know that I am "Always Never Alone."

"Have I not commanded you? Be strong and courageous. Do not be afraid; do not be discouraged, for the Lord your God will be with you wherever you go" (Joshua 1:9, NIV).

It is through brokenness that God's glory shines the brightest. It is not by our own strength that we can live, but through the grace and power of God that abides within each and every one of us.

I still have trials, still have moments where the enemy puts doubts in my mind and starts putting me down, but I know in those moments that I can fully put my trust in God, that He will be there to sustain me, to refresh me and be My Rock.

It is the Holy Spirit that empowers, strengthens, and gives us that inner peace and joy that this world will never give. We will all have trials and experience pain in our lives, but when we walk with the Holy Spirit, He enables us to face, go through and overcome the storms that come our way. When we keep our hearts aglow with God, nothing will be able to break us in this world. This might seem difficult to comprehend, but continuously being filled by the Holy Spirit, day by day, enables us to stand strong no matter the circumstances that come our way. Keep reading God's Word, keep meeting Him in that place of quietness, worship Him in song, for it is there that God will make His presence known to you. It says in **Psalms 22:3, KJV** that **"God inhabits the Praises of His People,"** and in **Psalm 47:6, "Sing praises to God, sing praises: Sing praises unto our King, sing praises."** When we humble ourselves and surrender our hearts, He begins to fill us with His Spirit.

The world and all that it had to offer did not give me that inner peace and joy. It is when God made His presence known to me that I realized that He was all that I needed. This indescribable peace that He gives is what I long to have for the rest of my life. I long for His presence, His love.

David once said: "Do not cast me from your presence or take your Holy Spirit from me" (Psalm 51:11, NIV). David knew that he could not function without the Holy Spirit. He needed Him as much as the air that he breathed. So should it be with every Believer.

When I had a personal three-hour encounter with God, it changed me forever. It was the first time in my life that I heard the Holy Spirit speak audibly to me, and the first time in my life that I encountered such deep intimacy with God with the Holy Spirit. I was filled with the power of the Holy Spirit, such as what happened at Pentecost in the upper room. I was put afire for Christ, filled with God's immeasurable love, joy and peace. No words can ever fully describe such an experience, but it it is for every Believer. All you need to do is ask God to fill you with the Holy Spirit, and He will.

"God wants us to experience over and over again the fresh outpouring of the Holy Spirit in our lives so that we can continue to do what He calls us to do with confidence and assurance."
—Mark Wixson–The Spirit of Christ Church —

Your journey—and my journey—is not done! God has a purpose for each one of us, but time is of the essence for Believers to be fully equipped, fully immersed by the mighty power of God. It is with a sense of urgency that God put upon my heart to share my story. I believe that now, more than ever, we need to be fully grounded in the Word. We need to know the voice of the Holy Spirit and the many ways He communicates with us. We need to be led by Him, moment by moment, to be fully anchored in God's love to withstand the storms ahead.

I believe that God's glory (power) will fall on this generation of Believers with an intensity that has never been seen before. Many will see the glorious manifestations of the presence of God and souls will be redeemed as they come to the knowledge of what Christ has done for them. Many Believer's hearts will be afire, totally yielded to accomplish, fulfill the calling that God has put upon their hearts. One soul that is saved can create a ripple that can impact a family, impact a city, impact a country, impact a nation!

God personally knows each one of us, for it states in the Word that He knew you before you were born **(Jeremiah 1:5)**. We all have a purpose, a calling, but we need to draw closer to God to know what He desires of us. God wants a personal relationship with you. He loves you so much. He will move heaven and earth to get your attention, to draw you to Him. And in that closeness, you will know that you are "Always Never Alone."

I will continue to lift my voice and raise my hands in worship to a King who has set me free. My heart afire, I will continue to praise Him, even amidst the storms.

"TO SEE YOUR EYES"

Lord, all I see is you, my Redeemer
I want to praise, worship you
Renew this battled mind
Please light the fire of my first love
My love for You

Let me walk with Holy fear, take Your Word
Be a light unto this world
Not just seek a crown, but give You the Glory
For the rest of my life, of my life

To see Your Eyes, to hear You say:
"I love you my child," as I fall to Your feet
In the presence of Your Glory, Your Glory

My body's getting old, I am weary
Let me keep the faith, finish the race
Let me remember what You did for me
As I close my eyes one last time

To see Your Eyes, to hear You say:
"Well done my child," as I fall to Your feet
In the presence of Your Glory, Your Glory

Copyright 2021, CC Harvey Music.

ACKNOWLEDGEMENTS

I would like to acknowledge the Holy Spirit who has been my constant companion. This book was created because of Him, and I give God all the Glory!

I would like to thank from the bottom of my heart those who have been there for me on this roller coaster of a journey:

My husband Peter, my best friend, who for the past three years has nudged me along to finish writing this book. You bring out the best in me and have always encouraged me to pursue God's calling. I am so blessed to have you in my life! Your unwavering love has been my anchor!

My son John and daughter KD who have brought me so much joy and fulfillment. May this book be a constant reminder of God's love for you!

My sister for encouraging me to write my story without fear. Thank you for sharing your knowledge of the Word and helping me grow.

My cousin Gerianne who has been there for me through the ups and down of writing this book. Thank you for your prayers, your counsel, your support and all the wonderful conversations we've had about the Holy Spirit.

My parents for always believing in me, encouraging me through all my journeys. Your love for each other has inspired me, both as a mother and as a wife.

My Aunt Yvonne, such a faithful servant of God, thank you for your prayers throughout the years and always being there for me.

Marilyn and all the ladies of our bible study group. You have blessed me with your love and friendships. You are all a true reflection of God's love and grace.

Pastor Mark Wixson of Spirit of Christ Ministries for his Godly counsel and help through some of the most challenging parts of this book. Pastor Mark passed away May 13, 2022. He was not only my mentor, but a good friend. I will miss him dearly.

Everyone on social media. Thank you for your prayers and encouragement throughout this journey. You have been such a blessing! Thank you for being a part of God's Kingdom work. May God bless you, fill you with his love and peace!

ABOUT THE AUTHOR

CC is a Singer/Songwriter, Recording Artist, Videographer, Author, and Speaker.

As the founder of CC Harvey Ministries, CC has been graced by God to empower Believers to walk victoriously in the anointing power of the Holy Spirit. Through personal testimony, CC shares how she faced and overcame many trials in her life with the help of the Holy Spirit.

At the age of seventeen, CC started singing in church and throughout her life has shared many messages in song given to her by the Holy Spirit. She presently ministers through zoom and is available to speak at various events.

By the grace of God, she received two nominations from the Canadian Gospel Music Association in 2021 for "Rock Song of the Year," and "Indigenous Song of the Year."

CC lives with her husband of over thirty years in Timmins, Ontario. Both of their children are now adults and have been blessed with wonderful careers: John in finance and KD in Nursing. Peter and Carmen are Grandparents to a beautiful baby boy, Felix who was born July 21st, 2021, to John and his wife Tina.

CC HARVEY MINISTRIES

"CC Harvey Ministries" is a department of A.C.T. International (Artist in Christian Testimony). A.C.T. International is an organization that helps equip and mobilize artists to spread the gospel of Jesus Christ to the world through music, art, and other media. Being a part of ACT international gives us credibility. It allows us to have a platform by which we can receive donations both in Canada and the United States to further the work that God has put upon our hearts.

Great things in ministry are not done by one person. They are done by a team of people working together towards one common goal, reaching souls for the Kingdom of God.

To book CC to speak at your next event, conference, zoom, or podcast go to:

www.ccharveyministries.com

Thank you for Reading my Book! Can You Help?

It would be so awesome if you could leave a review about "Always Never Alone" on Amazon.

If you enjoyed reading this book, your feedback would be really appreciated and would encourage others to read it as well and be blessed.

Thank you so much!

-CC Harvey -

"WHAT WILL YOU DO IF YOU ARE LEFT BEHIND"

(Behind the Scenes)

To view our ministry website please scan QR code. To view our end-time video and access some behind the scenes photos please visit this link:

https://www.ccharveyministries.com/end-time-ministry